"Terry's personal warmth stems from his obvious love of Jesus Christ and of God's children, all of them. His practical wisdom stems from his experienced capacity to listen and observe. I would have loved being a member of Terry's congregation. Here is a treasure trove of good counsel by a deeply consecrated priest for his fellow clergy, as useful as a handbook."

—ANDREW C. MEAD
Rector emeritus, Saint Thomas Church, New York City

"I worked with Terry for almost twenty-five years. . . . I found him to be a lovely and sincere man, very heartfelt, who built a wonderful congregation around his sermons and his concern for others, often more than himself. His book will touch anyone who reads it, and his presence and writing cannot help but inspire people to do their best within their spiritual tradition!"

—ANTHONY NEWMAN
Recording artist, Columbia Records, and world-renowned organist,
harpsichordist, composer, and conductor

"Gleaned from decades of ministry in a variety of church settings and illustrated by anecdotes from his own experience, the wisdom of Terry's advice about a distinctively pastoral style of congregational leadership is practical, clear, very engaging, and indispensable. Were I just graduated from seminary and entering a position on a church staff, I would be desperately looking for just this book!"

—DAVID H. KELSEY
Luther A. Weigle Professor emeritus of Theology, Yale Divinity School

"Drawing on real-life situations, Terry provides insight into how a leader can respond wisely, compassionately, and effectively. In my diocese, we encourage clergy to work collaboratively and meet in support groups. *Leading with Love* is ideal for these groups, and for anyone who is curious about how to address church situations which are complex but open to the Spirit. And it is perfect for new clergy."

—DOUGLAS FISHER
Bishop, Episcopal Diocese of Western Massachusetts

"Drawing on years of experience, this wonderful book offers us pragmatic and doable guidance on how to be a responsible and responsive church leader. Filled with anecdotes and practical examples and tackling the pitfalls as well, this book is a huge gift for anyone seeking to develop the skills of healthy, engaged, and—most of all—loving church leadership. It is a gift which will certainly keep on giving!"

—MARY D. GLASSPOOL
Assistant Bishop, the Episcopal Diocese of New York

"Terry delivers a book rich in leadership and life lessons for a broad audience. His counsel and advice are directly applicable to those charged with responsibility for communities of faith. But the questions he posits and the answers he provides . . . are relevant to all who are in positions of leadership anywhere in our society. This book is a compelling and insightful read."

—GREGORY FLEMING
Chief Executive Officer, Rockefeller Capital Management

LEADING WITH LOVE

LEADING WITH LOVE

Essentials of Church Leadership

By

TERENCE L. ELSBERRY

Foreword by Ian S. Markham

CASCADE *Books* • Eugene, Oregon

LEADING WITH LOVE
Essentials of Church Leadership

Cascade Books
An Imprint of Wipf and Stock Publishers
199 W. 8th Ave., Suite 3
Eugene, OR 97401

www.wipfandstock.com

PAPERBACK ISBN: 978-1-6667-2898-9
HARDCOVER ISBN: 978-1-6667-2085-3
EBOOK ISBN: 978-1-6667-2086-0

Cataloguing-in-Publication data:

Names: Elsberry, Terence L., author. | Markham, Ian S., foreword writer
Title: Leading with love : essentials for church leadership / Terence L. Elsberry ; with a foreword by Ian S. Markham.
Description: Eugene, OR: Cascade Books, 2021.
Identifiers: ISBN 978-1-6667-2898-9 (paperback) | ISBN 978-1-6667-2085-3 (hardcover) | ISBN 978-1-6667-2086-0 (ebook)
Subjects: LCSH: Christian leadership | Leadership | Pastoral theology | Church management
Classification: BV652.1 E47 2021 (paperback) | BV652.1 (ebook)

12/09/21

For the glory of God,

for the building up of his church,

and for

my wife, Nancy

"Then I will give you shepherds after my own heart, who will feed you on knowledge and understanding."

—Jeremiah 3:15

"But you are a chosen race, a royal priesthood, a holy nation a people for God's own possession, that you may proclaim the excellencies of him who has called you out of darkness into his marvelous light."

—1 Peter 2:9

"For just as we have members in one body and all the members do not have the same function, so we, who are many, are one body in Christ, and individually members of one another."

—Romans 12:4–5

"Go forth and set the world on fire!"

—Ignatius of Loyola

CONTENTS

Foreword by Ian S. Markham | xiii
Introduction | xv

PART 1: STARTING OUT

QUESTION 1
How did you prepare to be a rector or church leader? | 3

QUESTION 2
How should I analyze a call? | 11

QUESTION 3
What are the first things I should do? | 13

QUESTION 4
How do I connect with as many people as possible? | 15

QUESTION 5
How do I connect with parishioners in public situations? | 17

QUESTION 6
What's my first step in charting a course for my church? | 21

QUESTION 7
What should I NOT do in my first year? | 25

QUESTION 8
What about housing? | 28

QUESTION 9
How do I manage start-up details? | 29

QUESTION 10
How do I relate to the chief lay leader? | 32

QUESTION 11
How do I plan my weeks? | 33

QUESTION 12
How do I handle a problem that was not revealed
during the search process? | 35

QUESTION 13
Should I focus only on areas of parish life that interest me? | 38

QUESTION 14
I feel lonely. I'm afraid it may adversely affect my ministry.
What should I do? | 39

PART 2: LEADERSHIP

QUESTION 15
How can I become a better leader? | 43

QUESTION 16
What's the key to church leadership? | 48

QUESTION 17
What traits should a clergy leader cultivate? | 50

QUESTION 18
How can I juggle so many demands? | 55

QUESTION 19
What are recurring themes in church leadership? | 57

QUESTION 20
How do I formulate a vision? | 65

QUESTION 21
How do we determine priorities when funds are scarce? | 71

QUESTION 22
How do I do long-range planning? | 73

QUESTION 23
Do I have to attend all lay leadership meetings and all parish
events? | 78

QUESTION 24
How can I stay fresh throughout my years in ministry? | 80

QUESTION 25
What are the characteristics of a healthy church? | 83

QUESTION 26
How can a church become unhealthy? | 88

PART 3: MANAGEMENT

QUESTION 27
How do I effectively manage staff? | 93

QUESTION 28
How do I manage clergy assistants? | 99

QUESTION 29
What are some tips on running a meeting? | 102

PART 4: PEOPLE

QUESTION 30
How do I deal with dismissive parishioners? | 107

QUESTION 31
I feel drawn to certain individuals and families more than others.
Is this normal? | 109

QUESTION 32
I seem to be experiencing some conflict with a parishioner.
How do I resolve it? | 111

QUESTION 33
I'm feeling myself being drawn into several pastoral situations that
are weighing heavily on my heart. How do I deal with them? | 113

QUESTION 34
What about my use of alcohol in social settings with parishioners
and at parish functions? | 115

QUESTION 35
One of my staff comes to me and says a parishioner is expressing
dissatisfaction with me. What do I tell them? | 116

QUESTION 36
As you look back, are there pastoral situations you feel you could
have handled better? | 117

QUESTION 37
How can my church welcome newcomers? | 120

QUESTION 38
How do I inspire parishioners to greater stewardship? | 125

QUESTION 39
How do I Inspire the congregation to greater outreach? | 129

QUESTION 40
Should I encourage small groups? | 133

QUESTION 41
What are pitfalls to avoid? | 135

QUESTION 42
What about my family? | 138

QUESTION 43
What is my spouse/partner's obligation to the church? | 141

QUESTION 44
How do I maintain the church's and my energy
over the long haul? | 143

QUESTION 45
What was the hardest thing you had to do as a pastor? | 147

PART 5: PREACHING AND SERVICES

QUESTION 46
How do I approach preaching? | 151

QUESTION 47
How do you preach on the special occasions?
Easter, Christmas, Maundy Thursday, Good Friday. | 158

QUESTION 48
What about baptisms, weddings, and funerals? | 162

QUESTION 49
Do the seasons of the church year make a difference? | 171

QUESTION 50
How can I make the seasons distinctive? | 174

QUESTION 51
What about preaching on national holidays? | 177

QUESTION 52
A parishioner has asked me to drive evil spirits from their home.
How should I respond? | 180

PART 6: LOOKING BACK / LOOKING FORWARD:
THE CHURCH'S PLACE IN THE WORLD

QUESTION 53
Looking back, how did you manage leaving? | 187

QUESTION 54
What would you have done differently? | 190

QUESTION 55
Is there a crisis you feel you averted by something you did? | 191

QUESTION 56
What have been the greatest joys of your ministry? | 194

QUESTION 57
Looking forward, how do we deal with the changing pace
of the church in today's culture? | 197

QUESTION 58
How can the church meet the crises of the times? | 203

Glossary of Terms | 213

FOREWORD

If you want advice in ministry, then go to someone who has done the work well and for many years. You want to seek out a person who has served in a variety of different ministry settings and in each one achieved significant acclaim. You want someone who tells you how it is—without endless qualifiers. And you want someone who helps to teach you the questions you should be asking.

The Rev. Terry Elsberry is an experienced Rector, who succeeded as a parish priest. He has, in this delightful book, distilled all that wisdom. Using the format of question followed by answer, the book ranges from the hard work of discernment all the way through to the dismissive parishioner. Tips on managing staff and running a meeting sit alongside fascinating insights into preaching and wisdom about an appropriate departure.

The Terry Elsberry that you encounter in this book is a deep person of faith. His sense of call, his love of God, and his deep commitment to the people of God come pulsating through these pages. At various points, a Rector might want to quarrel with this or that detail, but everyone can learn with the simple clarity of vocation. In the disagreement with a parishioner, Terry Elsberry tells the reader to sit for a while with your Lord and seek to understand the disagreement. In the moments when ministry is hard, Terry Elsberry tells the reader to trust in the sense of call.

There are many obsolete religions in the world. And the reason for their demise is always the same. People stopped gathering. The gift of this book is that Terry Elsberry is seeking to help future clergy to ensure that the act of gathering as a congregations remains life-giving and life-enhancing. This volume can really help support effective congregational leadership. It is an extraordinary book written by an extraordinary priest.

The Very Rev. Ian S. Markham, Ph.D.
Dean and President
Virginia Theological Seminary

INTRODUCTION

Great news! You've completed the interviews. You've waited and wondered and hoped and prayed. The call has finally come. They want you. You feel like you're ready. Or you hope you are. Your starting date has been set. You've got to deal with the logistics of moving, along with breaking the news to the church you're currently serving and the often-excruciating emotions involved with saying goodbye. You're trying to be sensitive to the needs of your family, if you have one, who are being uprooted from home, church, community, and—maybe—jobs. With those wrenching things out of the way, and the move accomplished, you're left with the start-up. Excitement. Hope. Anticipation. Anxiety. Sometimes fear, even panic. Can I do it? Will I measure up? What if it doesn't work out? What if I—what if they—have made a mistake? What if I'm not a fit after all? How do I know if this is really a call or just wishful thinking on my part? Worst of all, what if I fail? Help, Lord!

I experienced all these feelings when I started at St. Matthew's, the church I served as rector for twenty-three years. St. Matthew's is an Episcopal Church in Bedford, New York, a small, historic, and picturesque town an hour by train to Grand Central station in New York City. Upon arrival, I felt as prepared as I could be, having served as clergy associate and before that as a seminarian in three churches where I was fortunate to understudy three highly talented and seasoned rectors. But when faced with the reality that now I was the clergy person in charge, I thought of all kinds of questions I wished I'd asked when I had the chance. This book comes as a response to actual questions asked me by clergy colleagues I've worked with through the years. Many are the same questions I've sought answers to in my own ministry. Each focuses on a discrete aspect of ministry. I'm sharing with you the distilled lessons of many years—lessons learned from my own successes and failures. I'm an Episcopalian, but I'm writing this not only for clergy of my denomination. Most of the things I've learned about leading a church apply to church leaders of all denominations. Whether you are, as I was, a rector or known as pastor, senior pastor, senior minister, elder, preacher, or by some other designation, these truths hold. This is no learned treatise, based on in-depth research of the American church today, although I've kept abreast of the trends—both hopeful and distressing—through the years.

Instead, I offer here a handbook, based on my thirty-plus years of parish ministry. Consider it a "How-to-do-it" based in large part on "How I've-done it." Though I've obviously geared at least the opening material to starting-up church leaders, much of what I've included here can apply to your ministry at whatever stage you're in. Here you'll find things I've learned, some negative, mostly positive, on how with the help and guidance of the Holy Spirit I've been able to lead and build a church. May you benefit from what I've learned. May the Lord bless your ministry as he has mine.

Terry Elsberry

PART 1

STARTING OUT

QUESTION 1

HOW DID YOU PREPARE TO BE A RECTOR OR CHURCH LEADER?

I'D BEEN PREPARING FROM THE TIME I LEFT SEMINARY

From the time I received my call, I knew I wanted to be a rector someday. I had no idea when, or how long it might take, but I felt strongly that was my ultimate call. Not to be a chaplain. Not to be a bishop. I wanted to be one of the Lord's "under shepherds," called by him, delegated by him, to lead, teach, nurture, care for, and love the flock chosen for me by him.

It took ten years from graduating from Virginia Seminary to starting as rector of St. Matthew's Church in Bedford, New York. In that time, I did these things to get ready:

I LEARNED EVERYTHING I COULD FROM THE RECTORS I SERVED.

Never underestimate the importance of mentors. I was remarkably fortunate in mine.

During seminary, as a seminarian for historic Christ Church in Old Town Alexandria, Virginia, my supervisor was Mark Anschutz. A third-generation rector, Mark galvanized what had been a rather sleepy parish into a powerhouse of Holy Spirit activity. Along with remarkable growth in numbers, he also inspired spiritual growth.

During my years as seminarian, I saw how a historic church with monuments to figures such as George Washington (who was on the vestry when the church was built in the late 1700s), and long-time parishioner Robert E. Lee (his monument has since been removed) could also thrive and flourish in today's world.

The worship was moving. The gospel was preached with integrity and power. Christian community was encouraged and developed with a variety of small-group programs. The poor and underprivileged were helped. And Mark taught his seminarians some crucial fine points of ministry.

Some I still remember and have used: Always take time for parishioners. Learn their names as fast as you can. Don't preach controversial subjects. As rector, it's your personal warmth, energy, drive, personality, and vision that can make or break a parish. Unexpected detail: use mouth wash. Mark always had a supply of mouthwash in the clergy bathroom for us to use right before a service.

My first position out of seminary was as assistant to John Harper, rector of St. John's Lafayette Square. Called "The Church of the Presidents," it had been built by a decree of Congress at the request of President James Madison so that he and Dolly could walk to church. St. John's is nationally known for the prayer service traditionally conducted there for presidents immediately before their inaugurations.

Here I was dealing with street people during the week and senators, congressmen and congresswomen, CIA and other professionals on Sundays. I quickly learned the importance of being able to deal effectively with all kinds of people.

When I was called to St. John's one of my seminary professors said, "Congratulations! In John Harper, you'll be working for the finest clergy administrator in the Episcopal Church."

From day one, I was impressed by John's skill in all the most important aspects of parish ministry. His remarkable attention to detail permeated every aspect of parish life at St. John's. Excellence was the byword. His philosophy was: it's better to do less if by doing more you relax your standards.

Key bases were covered—by him, by his lay staff, and by his two clergy associates. To this day I agree with John's priorities: worship, preaching, teaching, pastoral care, and mission . . . in this case to the then great number of homeless in downtown Washington.

John taught me, among other things, to develop a "style" of doing things that suits you as rector and the people you serve.

Here are some examples: St. John's parishioners liked to think and discuss, so we taught and led adult Christian Ed. classes that emphasized ideas and allowed plenty of time for discussion. Without overdoing it, John kept before the people their unique place as members of a church tied so closely with our nation's past and presently unfolding history. He gave great care and attention to carefully planned, crafted, and enacted liturgy. Pastoral care was consistent and loving.

John to me: "Black shoes with vestments and when you're sitting in a worship service, both feet on the floor." Then there's: "Never look out at the parishioners during the service; only eye contact is when you're preaching or administering communion." Speaking of detail: "When you're giving the announcements and final blessing, make sure you're standing in the center."

Other things John taught me include: Details are crucial. If you can't do it well, don't do it. In other words, don't tackle so many programs that you move beyond your effectiveness. When it comes to new initiatives, try only what has been thoroughly vetted by the people in charge. And know your people well enough to know they'll want what you offer.

He also had a dress code for us clergy (remember this was The 1980s a block from the White House) which had us wearing a suit every day. John's rationale? We should dress like our parishioners.

After two years, I went to Christ Church in Greenwich, Connecticut. Then the largest Episcopal church in the Diocese of Connecticut, it's situated on the main east/west street near the center of town. Which meant that there were activities—the church's and those of organizations that rented space in the church—seemingly day and night seven days a week. When I first arrived, I felt like I'd leapt aboard a freight train going at full speed and was hanging on for dear life.

The rector, Jack Bishop, was a powerhouse. He was a driving force for program and lots of it. Hard-driving, hard-working, high energy, he—like Anschutz and Harper—expected the best from his clergy and lay staffs. He had a particular gift for identifying and releasing talent in his people. He reminded us that no one has all the gifts. He hired clergy who balanced his skills. He showed me how important energy and dynamism can be in leading a parish. New initiatives flourished under his leadership.

Details of ministry I learned from Jack were the importance of getting parishioners to wear name tags at all church functions; setting chairs for every meeting and teaching in circles, not rows; and paying attention to process (example: when leading a discussion group, make sure you give everyone who wants to a chance to share; but not for too long).

He said clergy should never let their parishioners know we're feeling sick, tired, or over-worked; *our* problems are never *their* problems.

He'd say, "Never underestimate the ignorance of the average church-goer. They haven't been to seminary. They don't know things we clergy take for granted. So, teach, teach, teach. Take every opportunity you can to explain why we're here, what it means to be the church." When it comes to offering a new adult education program, he'd say, "Make sure you're not answering a question nobody's asking." In other words, do your ground work. He also felt that feedback, which he enjoyed giving, was important; I liked this less than some of his other guidelines.

Looking back, I recall Jack's most oft-repeated, tactical guideline. Always be proactive, don't wait for things to happen, *make* them happen.

In all three rectors, I can report deriving some negative as well as positive learning; I vowed certain things I would never do. But the good far outweighed the bad. Consider your mentors. Study what they do and how they do it. And don't be afraid to ask questions.

I READ BOOKS ABOUT WHAT MAKES HEALTHY, FLOURISHING, SUCCESSFUL CHURCHES.

I still have some of those books. One thing I determined early in my research was that should God make me a rector, I would seek his help in growing the church, but not in numbers only. Cancer is growth. Attempting growth *for growth's sake*, paying too much attention to growing in numbers, can lead to neglecting other key areas of ministry. Just as our physical bodies need health for us to function at our best, so what the body of Christ—the local church—needs is also health. The Lord is here to help us achieve it.

From that moment of realization, my reading, prayer, and study focused on what it might mean for a church to actually be healthy. In your reading, try to be guided by the Holy Spirit. Depending on your previous training, personality, and the church you serve, some books will be more helpful than others.

I VISITED OTHER HEALTHY CHURCHES.

When Jack Bishop offered me the chance to take a short sabbatical, I jumped at the chance. He let me decide what to do. I booked meetings with churches I'd heard of that seemed from the outside to possess those traits I was learning to value.

I would visit flourishing, healthy churches. I'd served in three. Now I visited five more: Trinity Copley Square, a big, historic Episcopal church in the heart of Boston; St. Columba's Episcopal Church, more suburban in nature, in Washington, DC; Mount Paran Church of God, a huge charismatic/Pentecostal church in northside Atlanta; Trinity Wall Street by virtue of its lucrative land holdings in downtown New York City, the wealthiest Episcopal church in the nation; and what was then the largest Protestant church in America, Willow Creek, in South Barrington, Illinois, west of Chicago.

WHEN THE CALL CAME FROM ST. MATTHEW'S, I LEARNED EVERYTHING ABOUT IT I COULD IN THE SHORT TIME AVAILABLE

I took the clergy to lunch individually. They were the interim minister, the former rector's associate, and the deacon. I could not have met with a more dissimilar bunch. The first two complained about what they didn't like about the church. Neither had one positive thing to say. I never met with them again. By the time I started as rector, they'd moved on.

The deacon, a lovable guy twenty years older than I, stayed on. Happily, for me and for the church. His name was Broaddus ("Speed") Johnson. He'd been a member of St. Matthew's for forty years, becoming a deacon after a successful career in TV advertising. He knew the church thoroughly. His opinions, stories, and deep understanding of the St. Matthew's ethos proved invaluable for all the years we served together, which turned out to be many. Over time, I'd run new ideas and initiatives by him. Most of them he affirmed. But if in his seemingly offhand way, he'd say, "I think you'd make more friends if you didn't try that one" I didn't.

From all three—interim, associate, and deacon—I *did* get the crucial information: the names of parishioners who would need my initial pastoral attention.

I also re-read the parish profile and the published history of the church, which began with the beginning—in the 1600s, when Anglicans met in homes locally—and concluded in 1960. One of my first initiatives was to update the history, written by a parishioner who doubled as church historian. You'll find in your new church situation the same attention to learning about the past will show your people you really care about their church and them.

I PRAYED FOR ST. MATTHEW'S

I began praying for the church and for its people from the day I received the call. I prayed for them during the twenty-three years I served as their rector. I've prayed for them since I left. I will pray for them always.

THEN THERE'S THE PRE-SEMINARY PREPARATION I UNWITTINGLY CHOSE BUT FOUND USEFUL

The pastor of my boyhood church was Lester Proctor. He taught me the value of grace in adversity and the unfailing cheerfulness that seemed to propel him through life.

Along with what I unconsciously learned from him and from my ardently Christian, staunchly church-going parents, and from going to church my whole life (even while in college), I also had the following experiences that have proven useful. They all took place during my early thirties.

I spent three months working in a ministry to street people in inner-city Baltimore. I lived in a third-story walk-up, with a lock at every level. The complex included a church, a thrift shop, and a so-called turn-around home for young men getting out of rehab programs or jail. The program's goal was to mainstream the men by giving them job-skill training and helping them get, and keep, jobs.

Church services on Wednesday and Sunday mornings featured hard-sell gospel messages to locals, some of whom were homeless. Every service was concluded with hands-on, individual prayer and lunch.

I grew up in small-town Iowa, later lived and worked in prosperous suburbs. I'd never experienced real poverty close-up, had no idea of the incredible number of advantages I'd always taken for granted.

My three months in the inner city changed my life. I developed a heart for urban ministry. God hasn't called me to parishes in disadvantaged areas. So my goal has been to inspire parishioners in every church I've served to find concrete ways to help the disadvantaged.

If Jesus is present in the life of a church, it must make a difference in the lives of those who need our help.

8

A MISSION TRIP TO JAMAICA PROVED TO BE ANOTHER UNWITTING PREPARATION FOR WHAT LAY AHEAD

Here's how it happened. A retired U. S. missionary to Jamaica took a group of us young men who'd had either a conversion or other kind of dramatic spiritual experience.

He said a lot of the young people he'd worked with while in Jamaica had been active in church when young. But now, as young adults, they'd fallen away. His goal was to take us to churches, after a lot of advance planning, and share personal testimonials of our life-changing experiences with the Lord.

I'll never forget preaching (I who had never preached) to a packed church high in the Blue Mountains of Jamaica. That experience taught me two things. One, that with God's help you really can do anything. Two, when it comes to delivering a word God has given you—and he certainly did give me his word that night—age, nationality, skin color, cultural background mean nothing. What matters is that we are all the people of God and precious in his sight.

The longer you serve the more you'll realize all kinds of unconscious preparation the Lord has been doing all your life completely without your awareness. It was true for me. It's true for you. Expect to suddenly draw on certain past experiences—some you may have even forgotten—when you need them.

I GAVE IT TO THE LORD

In my early thirties I had a life-changing spiritual experience that resulted from my surrendering my life to God.

During all the years since, I've tried to stay in that surrendered attitude. Sometimes with more difficulty than other times.

When I was ordained, I applied that same attitude of submission to the Holy Spirit to my ministry. Thus, when I became rector, I surrendered my St. Matthew's ministry to him. I asked him to show me his plan and guide me along the way. Every idea I had, every meeting I led, every sermon I preached, every class I taught and ministry activity I carried out, began first with my praying for God's input, God's wisdom, and guidance.

And I taught the people of St. Matthew's that when it comes to building the church "Lest the LORD builds the house; they labor in vein that build it" (Psalm 27:1).

I *did* ask the Lord one question repeatedly for the first several weeks I was rector. I kept praying, "Lord, what have you brought me here to do? Is there any special assignment you have for me here?"

I prayed the same prayer over and over. No answer came. Finally, one day as I walked from the rectory to my office in the parish house, the words ran through my mind: "Bloom where you're planted."

After that I relaxed. I took those words to mean that God would show me what to do as I moved forward day by day. And he did.

He did it for me. He'll do it for you. But it's important to give, release, surrender it to him—whatever "it" is. Make trust in his personal involvement a functional cornerstone of your ministry. Get "self" out of the way and let God guide you as you go. That's how great things can happen.

QUESTION 2

HOW SHOULD I ANALYZE A CALL?

ASK QUESTIONS

Ask the Lord. Ask him to show you, make it undeniably clear to you, if it's his will for you to take this call—or not. It may look right on the surface, but *is* it right for you, for your family, and for the church *now*? Only God knows. If necessary, ask him for a sign, a "fleece." You don't want to miss the Lord on this; there's too much at stake.

Ask your interviewers. Ask as many questions as you can of the people you interview with. Looking back on my interview process with St. Matthew's, I realize I wanted the call so badly I didn't ask enough questions. I was too eager to be liked and wanted by them. Fortunately, it was the right place for me. But if it hadn't been, I would have suffered the consequences. So would my wife. So would the church. So ask questions.

Ask your mate (if you have one). I was fortunate here. The Lord showed Nancy before he showed me that St. Matthew's was the place for us. She said: "The Lord has showed me we're going to St. Matthew's." I clung to that when, for a time, it looked like it wasn't going to happen.

Ask yourself: "Can I love these people? Do they have needs I can meet?"

Before I became rector, my name was in three other searches. But from the beginning, I had a special liking for the St. Matthew's people, a unique affinity for them. As sometimes happens when you meet the person of your dreams, I loved them on sight!

I also instinctively felt I could help them meet certain needs that had gone unmet for a long time.

St. Matthew's had many attributes, many assets. What I felt it needed was a leader to breathe life into the system. It could use an injection of Vitamin B. It was as if the place was slumbering. I thought of a princess sleeping under the influence of a spell. All she needed was someone to give her a kiss and bring her back to life. The people needed a shepherd who would love them, remind them of how great they were, show them the great things they could do.

When preparing for your new position, ask yourself what are the primary needs here?

QUESTION 3

WHAT ARE THE FIRST THINGS
I SHOULD DO?

INTERACT WITH THE PEOPLE — INDIVIDUALLY

A lot of starting-up rectors have asked me the same question: what's the most important thing for me to do? Every time my answer has been the same: *love the people*. Like it or not, for many of our parishioners, at some subliminal level for them, you and I are stand-ins for the Lord. At the very least we are his representatives. In his relationship with us, he always leads with love. So must we. (Even when we may sometimes have to grit our teeth to do it!)

This mantra, "love the people," has been for me the foundation for all I've done as a parish priest—both at the beginning and during my ministries in a variety of parishes. Love is the greatest power in the world. Love is why God sent his Son to die in our place.

The reason I love being a parish priest so much is because there are so many people to love.

And what happens when for whatever reason you don't feel very loving? That's when you pray, when you say, "God, love this person *through* me."

The primary importance of love in ministry is why from the beginning we seek out those who are hurting the most—physically, emotionally, relationally, financially, in whatever way.

We need to connect with them as soon as is feasibly possible: a phone call, visit, note. Find out from the people on the search committee, existing staff—clergy or lay—who these people are, then get to them. They'll feel cared for and all the people who are watching you (and that's a whole lot of

13

the church) will know you care. Which is a crucial first step in their ability to trust you.

GET TO THE OLDEST PEOPLE AS FAST AS YOU CAN

Why? Because they'll want to see who's going to bury them. Also, it's important that these elders who once played a leading role in the church and due to age or infirmity no longer can, still feel valued by their church and by you. Also, most of them will be eager to tell you their stories.

These visits, along with the joy of meeting some interesting and usually delightful characters, are crucial in helping you get to know your new church.

Ask these elders to tell you their stories of times past at this church you've just come to as their spiritual leader. They'll feel affirmed. They'll warm to recounting tales of times past. I've seen elderly parishioners actually lose years from their faces as they spark with the delight of recalling happy memories of their church.

The stories they tell you will prove invaluable as you begin to understand the culture of the church you've just walked in to. As leaders, we need to know our church's history. We are the latest in a chain, however long, of pastors who have been called by God to carry forth his vision for this particular, local expression of his Spirit at work in a community of believers. What a high calling it is!

SEEK OUT AND CONNECT WITH THE FORGOTTEN ONES

Forgotten? There are those members of every church who don't have the time, the energy, or the resources to live in the main flow of the church. Maybe they've been disaffected for some reason. Maybe, as one elderly lady told me, they for some reason have never felt like they quite "belonged" to the culture of the church community. Maybe they don't have much money and can't pledge and therefore feel guilty.

After you've been in place for a while, with the help of longtime lay leadership, begin to look for people who aren't very connected. Go to them. Get to know them. Make them feel important. These people may be invisible to the church, but they matter to God. They need to matter to us. Do your best to help them feel as important as the most visible leaders and the biggest givers.

QUESTION 4

HOW DO I CONNECT WITH AS MANY PEOPLE AS POSSIBLE?

LEARN NAMES

This can feel not only daunting. It can feel overwhelming. Especially if you're not naturally good with names.

I've always told my staffs that the two most important things for a parishioner to hear are Thank you and the sound of their own name.

There are guidelines for how to remember names. It helps me, when I'm meeting somebody for the first time, to use the new person's name more than once. If you're like me, you're so busy taking in the person's look and personality and making the initial small talk, that when he or she moves on you realize you don't have a clue what their name is. I make it a practice to repeat the name as often as time and reason permit. It helps ingrain the name.

Also, there may be someone else you know with the same name. Making that connection can help. If you're really feeling undone by the name game, and have the time, there are "How to Remember Names" courses available. However you manage it, it is *essential* you learn names—and quickly.

You also need to incorporate the wearing of name tags at every service and every event. Calling people by name as you administer communion to them has great meaning.

Not long ago, when we moved, I came across a little breast pocket notebook in one of my desk drawers. It was one I carried the first few months I was rector. I made a practice of leaving coffee hour after the main service and jotting down in the little book things I remembered about people I'd met—names, activities in the church, something I'd learned about their families. Having that little crib sheet was a great help in getting connected fast.

SAY THANK YOU

Showing appreciation is another way to forge early connections. A simple thank you is an invaluable bonding tool.

As I said earlier, I've duplicated a lot of things my clergy mentors taught me—successfully so. The few negative learnings have also proved valuable. One rector had the theory that he needn't thank parishioners for services they performed. His reason: serving God and his church were thanks enough.

I could not disagree more. The church is made up of volunteers. Many of them lead busy lives. To give themselves in serving the mission of the church sometimes takes them away from their families and other important activities or interests. Usually we'll never know what their serving the church may be costing them.

Thank them. Show them you value their contributions. As soon as you can, send them a hand-written note (doubly valued for how old-fashioned and rare it has become). Or an email, text, or phone call. Whatever seems appropriate. At the very least, thank them the next time you see them. Out of the blocks they'll feel valued by their new pastor and feel that in you they have a person they're glad to have leading their church.

Psychologists have actually studied the effects thank-you notes engender in their recipients. What they've discovered is that people love getting thank-you notes. (No surprise.) Studies also show that too many people underestimate the positive feelings their notes engender

QUESTION 5

HOW DO I CONNECT WITH PARISHIONERS IN PUBLIC SITUATIONS?

BE THE CHIEF ENCOURAGER

You need to start by building a positive climate. Church should be the most positive place in our lives. If the Spirit of God is present, then love, joy, and peace abound. All that and mutual appreciation.

In every institution and organization—certainly in church—much of the sense of the place, the feeling of connectedness, of community, starts at the top—with you. You are here to channel the persona of the Lord, the one who loves each of us absolutely and completely.

Encourage. Encourage. Encourage.

CONNECT WITH THE PEOPLE WHO MAKE THINGS HAPPEN

Connect with your worship leaders, staff—lay and clergy, and with your parish leadership, vestry or board members, and commission and/or committee chairs. They're all eager to find out who this character is who's been called as their new leader.

Early on, tell them enough things about yourself to help them know something about who you are. My parishioners knew from the beginning that I'm from Iowa, that I'd been in publishing and corporate communications, that I'm a New York Yankees and Green Bay Packers fan, an Anglophile, and that I adore my wife, children, grandchildren, beaches, and the theater.

IN YOUR SERMONS AND TEACHINGS, IN THE NEWSLETTER AND ON THE WEBSITE, PAINT A HOPEFUL FUTURE

Your new congregation needs to know you have positive plans for their church. Two rectors of the same church, called some twenty years apart, conveyed two very different initial messages.

The first, when asked by his vestry what plans he might have for the church, said, "I don't really have any plans. Guess I'll have to wait until I get there and see what's needed."

The second, from day one, began detailing positive new objectives. Of course, some things would change with time and as he got to know his new church better. But during the search process, by studying the materials and quizzing the people who'd interviewed him, he knew from the start some things that needed to be done.

The first indicated he didn't have an idea of where he might lead the church. A natural response from parishioners: if *he* doesn't know where we're going as a church, who does? Does he care?

The second started out modeling purpose—hope for a positive future, a plan to follow.

It's good to have a few set principles to set forth immediately—such as "I know with the Lord's help we're going to do great things together," and: "I'm excited to be here and excited about working with you to build our church."

I remember saying things like: "Come on! Get on board! We're going to do great things together. We can't see all those things yet. There are going to be some surprises as the Lord reveals his plan to us. And that's part of the excitement! We're on our way!"

Some of the staid traditionalists in the church weren't too sure what to make of this dude who'd become their rector. The majority of people indicated in various ways that they'd be with me all the way. And they were. So, too, were the initial nay-sayers.

The more positive the energy environment you create, the more effective you're going to be. You need to start convincing the people from Day One to get ready. Because you're going to have a wonderful new beginning. Whatever positive or negative experiences they may have been through as a church, you need to be all positive. Give them *hope*. Hope is contagious. People want to get on board and see what these exciting things might be.

You may not be completely sure yourself. It may be too early for many specifics to have surfaced. But you know God is faithful. You know he wants to help you help them be his church in this particular part of the world. Which means a church alive with Holy Spirit energy, dynamism, and a sense of adventure.

Of course, some building blocks are necessary in every church: inspiring preaching, strong teaching, pastoral care, compelling liturgy, a solid church school, lay ministry—both to people in need within the church and outside in the greater community, and a sense of excitement and fun about being in church together.

Over and over through the years, I kept telling them, "This is the best church in America." They knew that was open to discussion, subject to opinion, that I had my tongue partly in my cheek. But they took my hyperbole as proof of my dedication to the ministry we were carrying out together. And since I loved them so much, I actually couldn't imagine a better church.

REMEMBER: IT'S NOT ABOUT YOU

It's about God and his people. You've come to help the people strengthen and deepen that relationship, sensitive to where they are on their journey. As in all relationships, your listening is more important than your talking. Sometimes I've walked away from an interchange and thought, "I talked too much about myself."

I've known clergy with narcissistic tendencies who take every comment the other person makes to launch into a story about themselves. Someone should have told them not to do it. Sometimes it's okay to make a few personal comments. There's a place for mutual sharing. But our first call is to listen, to question, to seek parishioners out, to empathize, not to charm them with anecdotes about ourselves and our families. It's never, never about us, it's about *them*. You're here to hear about *them*. It's true from the day you arrive. It's true until the day you leave.

I read a book many years ago—I forget the title and the author—that made a classic analogy. The writer said that as newly arrived clergy leaders, we need to get in the boat with the people and go down the river looking at the shoreline through their eyes. What is their reality? What is their understanding of the meaning and purpose of the church in general and of their church in particular? That metaphor has stood me in good stead—not just at the beginning but through the years of a long-term ministry.

Remember: you may be the leader, but this is not *your* church first. It's the *Lord's* first and the *people's* second. We clergy come and go; the church will continue along its chosen path (which hopefully coincides with the Lord's plan) after we're gone just as it did before we arrived.

That doesn't mean we don't give it everything we have. We do. We must. God would have us prayerfully pour all our passion, energy, vitality, creativity, and commitment into this work he's given us to do. But too much ownership on our part can rob us of our objectivity.

QUESTION 6

WHAT'S MY FIRST STEP IN CHARTING A COURSE FOR MY CHURCH?

HONE THE VISION

The best way to begin this is by getting the parish leadership away on a weekend retreat as soon as possible after your arrival.

I'm a believer in annual retreats for the clergy and lay leaders of every church. A church without a clearly articulated, clearly understood vision will never become all it can be.

It's up to you as leader to convince your vestry or board how important this is. Some may see it as a waste of time. "We don't need a visioning conference. We know what the church is here for: worship God, preach the word, educate our children, help each other, help needy people.

They'd be right, of course. But just as we're all different, so the Lord calls every church to a particular expression of his mission to the world. The apostle Paul's comment that as evangelists we need to be all things to all people notwithstanding, as a local church we can't be all things to all people. No church can do everything. Just as no single person has all the gifts, so no local church has all the same strengths and talents.

When you plan your first visioning retreat, do these things: Pray earnestly for the Lord's revelation and guidance. Give each of your vestry or board members the opportunity to explain these things about their church: what drew them here, what they like best, what they'd like to see changed, improved, or enhanced, and finally . . .

BUILD ON STRENGTHS

Build on the existing strengths your new church *does* have, those traits that make your church unique. Every church, whatever the size, has certain special gifts. Identifying these key attributes and learning how best to express them are the key underpinnings of formulating the vision.

Presumably, the lay leadership have already been through a similar process in preparing the parish profile used in the search that brought you here. But it's a different experience now that you are here, and ready to lead them forward.

Thus, comes next the useful, fun, and freeing exercise of *dreaming*; ask them what they'd like their church to look like in five—in ten—years.

You should be able to leave this first retreat agreed on a handful of your church's primary strengths. Early on, I recognized that St. Matthew's had four that set it apart from other churches in the area. They were:

- One, *a unique history*, with John Jay as our so-called founding father and original senior warden (we had his warden's staff in a glass case just inside the front door).

- Two, *the church is remarkably attractive*—with a movie-set campus of beautiful, understated buildings and an unusually lovely graveyard, set on sixty-seven acres, most of it heavily wooded, with a stream, trails through the woods, and an outdoor chapel where in the summer we held early Sunday morning Communion services.

- Three, we had an unusually strong *family orientation*—with an excellent church school (and, later, a pre-school we started, which drew from the surrounding community) and such well-attended all-parish family events as The Haunted Hike and Spaghetti Supper, Mardi Gras, and, in June, an All-Parish Picnic.

- Four, *worship*. Carefully crafted, but simple and more "low church," than most of the Episcopal churches currently are, it was in keeping with the restrained English Reformation architecture. And we had tremendous support from our music—directed by our world-renowned organist and director of music, my dear colleague and friend, Anthony Newman.

- A fifth strength, our *commitment to outreach*, deepened over time.

Of course, we had other strengths, as every church does. But you need to identify, strengthen, and expand on those that are uniquely your church's and help your people do the same.

STRENGTHEN YOUR CHURCH'S IDENTITY

Also, a clear sense of identity—who we are, why we're here—is an important corporate point to make. And to keep making. You're branding!

For example: your mission statement. Every church needs one. The one we came up with during our first visioning retreat, kept all the years I was rector and that is still used since I've left: "To know Christ and to make him known."

We've all seen planning groups struggle for hours coming up with mission statements that, though important and representative of the church and its goals and ministries, are too long and complicated for anyone to remember! Keep your mission statement *short, concise, easy to memorize.* As somebody said, "Your mission statement should fit on the front of a sweatshirt."

And use it every chance you get—on your Sunday bulletins, your weekly and monthly newsletters, and everywhere else it seems feasible. Parishioners like to know they're part of a church with a strong identity.

Having devoted the time, energy, and dedication to learning the culture, it's now up to you to do your own culture creating. We build on the best of the past to move into an ever more positive future.

TEACH THE MEANING OF THE CHURCH

This is foundational. Many faithful Christians don't really understand what it means to be part of the body of Christ. Some have only a vague idea of the biblical teaching of what the church is and the part God calls us to play in the world around us.

With that in mind, the first fall I was at St. Matthew's, I taught a Wednesday night adult education series "What it Means to Be a Christian." Because my predecessor had been criticized for not opening the rectory to parishioners, I held the class in the rectory library. It was packed for every session. I discovered, happily, that a lot of my new parishioners were eager to know the meaning and importance of church and the role the Lord wants them to play as members of the local Christian community.

Building on that format, the following spring I did a follow-up class: "What it Means to Be an Episcopalian." This class was aimed at four groups of parishioners:

- New, non-Episcopal, members who wanted to learn more about the church they'd chosen to be a part of.

- Those long-time parishioners who had not been confirmed as a child and wanted to be confirmed now as adults.

- Long-time Episcopalians who had been confirmed but wanted to make a re-affirmation when the bishop came to confirm our class of thirteen-year-olds.

- The final group consisted of life-long Episcopalians who simply wanted to brush-up on the history and personality of Anglicanism.

When the bishop came to do confirmation, we had twenty adults who were either confirmed or re-affirmed their confirmation vows.

I suggest you teach similar classes for two reasons. First, I've always found the classroom setting, with plenty of Q. and A., a great opportunity for us to get to know our people better. At the same time, it's been my experience that with greater knowledge of the church and one's denominational expression of the faith comes deeper commitment.

WHAT SHOULD I *NOT* DO IN MY FIRST YEAR?

DON'T MAKE ANY MAJOR CHANGES

Some years ago, I attended a national pastors conference in a major city. The group was made up of pastors of large parishes, most of them endowed. These men and women would have been considered some of the most successful clergy in the nation.

But the only thing I remember from that long-ago conference is a conversation that took place one day at lunch. I was still a cub assistant, barely out of seminary. But I had the good fortune of finding myself at a table filled with several renowned rectors and two bishops.

To my amazement, and eager interest, their discussion—to which I was able to contribute nothing—focused not on their successes but on their failures. It turned out that both of the bishops had been bounced out of major big-city churches shortly after their arrival as rector.

Another, also a seasoned veteran, asked: "Why? What happened?" Both men, virtually in chorus, answered, "Because we made major changes in the first year."

It turned out that both men had unknowingly made changes that so enraged some parishioners they'd been asked to leave before they'd barely begun their tenure.

One man had removed an enormous cross that had hung over the main altar in a big downtown church. To his dismay, only when it was too late did he discover that the cross—though jarringly ugly to the rector— had been the gift of a founding family in honor of a much-loved family member. The parishioners loved it, ugly or not, because it reminded them of someone they'd valued and revered.

The discredited rector could have saved himself a lot of heartache—and his job—if he'd taken time to ask some questions; starting with something as basic as *not*, "What's the story on the hideous cross?" but more like, "Can you tell me the history of the cross?"

The other discredited rector had received his walking papers by coming into a low church with the set intention—not adequately conveyed to the people who interviewed and hired him—of turning the low church he signed on to lead into a high church.

At that, I remembered something my seminary liturgics professor, Charlie Price, a major contributor to the 1979 Book of Common Prayer, had said. He said, "When you change the way people worship, you're changing *them*. Most people aren't asking to be changed."

Remember that when you come new into your church: change nothing for the first year and after that change anything major only after carefully preparing the people who are going to be affected by the change. Those people may be only a segment of the church, or the whole church.

After only a few weeks of my boat ride down the river with my new parishioners, looking at the church through their eyes, I quickly understood there was one worship service I could never change, never even consider "tweaking." It was "The Manger Services." Held at four and six p.m. on Christmas Eve, these identical services had been, I was quickly informed, initiated by the then-rector at the end of the Civil War, in 1866. "And nothing about the service has changed since," I was firmly told by more than one of my new parishioners. "Nothing's changed. *Nothing*." And, I got the idea, nothing *would* be changed—not by me, not by any future potentially presumptuous rector.

(In fact, something *had* changed, but I never told anybody. I found an old, falling-apart order of service from the first ever service, in 1866, and though the form, outline, prayers, and Scripture readings were indeed still the same after all these years, I didn't recognize one carol they sang! Who knew they didn't sing all the same carols in 1866 that we sing today?)

Remember also: the laity have ownership. It's *their* church. Most of them love it because it's the way it is. Most of them aren't asking for changes; the world is changing so rapidly and for some in ways that feel so frightening, for a lot of your people their church is the safest place they have.

And safe to them means basically unchanging. Your number one take away needs to be: *No big changes in your first year.*

QUESTION 8

WHAT ABOUT HOUSING?

EVERY CHURCH HAS ITS OWN HOUSING SET-UP

And options are rare. Living in the rectory was part of my package. I've known other churches that give their rectors a housing allowance so they can choose their housing. Sometimes churches will help the rector buy a house. Both contribute to the down payment and gain the requisite percentage of return when the property sells.

Depending on your financial situation, if you can make it work, the third option seems the most advantageous.

Rectory living can be problematic. Having to call someone on the Property Commission every time you have a maintenance need gets old fast. You get the refrigerator they choose, the paint job when they think you need it.

I've sat in groups of clergy while they complained about how hard it was to get their churches to pop for rectory expenses.

Nancy's and my first major surprise after coming to our new church was waking up on an early Saturday morning in October to see men of the parish on the porch roof outside our bedroom windows. Fall cleanup. Volunteers cleaning the gutters. Somehow, I'd written down the wrong date for cleanup. It didn't happen again.

Over the long haul, though, the charm of the old rectory made up for the occasional frustrations that came with our lack of control. Memories of living in that old house will always be some of the best of my life.

QUESTION 9

HOW DO I MANAGE START-UP DETAILS?

DRESS ON THE JOB

Sunday morning: suit or sport jacket. My tradition: black shoes. And well-polished. I've had parishioners comment on my shoes. They see them clearly when kneeling for communion.

Weekday dress offers some variables. I've altered my weekday dress according to the guidelines of rectors I've served.

St. John's Lafayette Square was "low church" formal. We wore suits and ties during the week, except on days we wore clergy collars because we were doing a mid-week Communion service or funeral.

Christ Church Alexandria and Christ Church Greenwich: collars every day.

When I became rector of St. Mathew's, another low church, weekdays I wore a collar on days when leading liturgies. Otherwise: sport jacket and tie. Sunday was a suit, black shoes for John Harper, and a collar.

I know we're in the dress-down era. If you're in a community where it's acceptable for you to go without a jacket and tie and that's what you prefer, do it. I know I'm old-fashioned, but for a variety of reasons I felt the weekday necktie was right for the local culture. Keep in mind the dress codes of the community you serve. Whether you're female of male, serving a wealthy or poor community, be well-groomed, even on your day off. You may go around town in casual clothes, but never, never look grubby. You're representing your church. You're representing the Lord.

TIME OFF THE FIRST YEAR

Get vacation times settled and in your Letter of Agreement before you begin. The first year should be no different than every year thereafter. I always took a week after Christmas and Easter and a month in the summer. Days off were up to me, which meant I virtually never took an entire day off—which I do *not* recommend! When I'd been rector going on twenty years, I began also taking off Columbus Day and Presidents' weekends. But I was fortunate to have in-house assisting clergy coverage. When starting out, I felt I needed to prove to the church—and myself—that I could do the job. One thing that meant was I overworked, almost never took a day off in those first months, was exhausted by Christmas. *Don't* do what I did. Remember you're in it for the long haul. If God has called you to this place, he expects you to care for yourself and your family, so find your best ways to do it.

The Episcopal Church recommends sabbaticals every seven years. I had one as rector and took other study breaks as they seemed feasible—always planned in conversation with the vestry. Again: preparation is everything. Prepare your lay leaders and the congregation for where you're going and why you're going. When you return, report on what you've learned.

HONORARIA FOR PASTORAL SERVICES

These may be already set by local church and/or diocesan or national church traditions.

As rector, what I received for doing weddings, memorial services, and funerals went directly into my discretionary fund. I used this to help organizations and individuals. A church account, it was audited every year along with the rest of the church finances.

TIP. Be able to sign on only one church account: your discretionary. It's a fail-safe way to avoid ever getting into any kind of financial trouble.

EXPENSES

I've had it two ways. One, you keep track of your mileage and lunches you buy for parishioners and present documentation to the bookkeeper for reimbursement.

A better way, for me anyway, was to agree that as rector I'd receive a monthly allowance for car and household expenses and credit cards for gas and entertainment. I provided the bookkeeper with names and reasons for entertainment.

As with your vacation time, it's best to have management of your expenses settled before you begin.

QUESTION 10

HOW DO I RELATE
TO THE CHIEF LAY LEADER?

DEVELOP TRUST

I've heard horror stories of bad pastor–lay leader relationships. Probably you have too. Happily, that never happened to me. Every warden—both senior and junior—I had possessed markedly different personalities. But though I had occasional arguments, I never had any major conflicts with any of them.

You'll begin with the leaders who are in place. Presumably, they have a high regard for you or they wouldn't have called you in the first place.

You'll have an easier, more natural flow in relating with some, less so with others. But your goal needs to be finding ways to agree on how best to serve the church you both obviously deeply care for.

You need to listen carefully to them. Never override them unless you feel it's absolutely necessary. And never do it in a vestry meeting or in any other public venue.

One way to make sure that never happens is to do what I always did: meet with both wardens a few days before every vestry meeting to build the agenda and talk through the issues at hand. That way you can deal with any differences of opinion in advance in private.

And there's nothing wrong with the occasional disagreement. But as in every relationship, you need to work overtime building trust. Trust, as in every relationship, benefits not only you and your wardens. It benefits the church.

QUESTION 11

HOW DO I PLAN MY WEEKS?

HERE'S HOW I DID IT

I've always remembered what John Harper told me his mentor for ministry said to him: "Conduct business in the morning; do your calling in the afternoon."

With only some variance, I've always followed that format. Afternoons for me were unvaryingly devoted to pastoral care—hospital and nursing home visitation; visits with older parishioners; sometimes in-office pastoral counseling sessions. This format worked for me, my staff, and for the parishioners.

Monday morning, I met with my secretary to go over my calendar for the week. Every morning, of course, you have to check your phone and emails first thing, to make sure you haven't missed any crises.

Tuesday morning, to the above I added a clergy staff meeting to go over any pastoral issues and determine who would do what in the following Sunday services. Staff meetings, attended by clergy and lay, followed at ten a.m.

Wednesday morning I wrote my notice for the weekly, all-parish email (affectionately known in-house as "The Blast"), met with the secretary who put together the Sunday Order of Service, and often met with the parish administrator to confer over any administrative, financial, or staff concerns she might have.

Thursday mornings were more emails, calls, writing thank-you letters, and were usually followed by lunch with a parishioner—often a vestry member or other lay leader.

Friday morning, my "day off," I wrote my sermon for the upcoming Sunday. That left me time to mull over and edit for Sunday morning.

Saturdays were committee or commission meetings and/or pre-marital or pre-baptismal meetings.

Sunday mornings I was up at six, went over my sermon one last time, got to church *always* by seven-thirty for the eight o'clock service. I've known clergy who breathlessly rush in to lead liturgies at the last minute, leaving themselves and the other participants a little uptight and wired. I say: give yourself plenty of lead time, making it easier to deal with any last-minute problem that might emerge.

The eight o'clock over, I often met with my senior warden to discuss how things were going. Failing that, it was home to the rectory for a second jolt of coffee.

Then off to the main, ten o'clock, service followed by coffee hour in the parish house. After coffee hour and before lunch, I'd make the twelve-mile trip to the hospital if we had anyone there. If not, it was home, lunch, and a nap!

You'll find, with time, what works best for you. Some of what will determine your daily planning will depend on your energy levels (higher in the morning or afternoon) and the requirements of your staff and planning schedules.

QUESTION 12

HOW DO I HANDLE A PROBLEM THAT WAS NOT REVEALED DURING THE SEARCH PROCESS?

SLOWLY, CAREFULLY, AND PRAYERFULLY

Of course, there will be one or several such issues. It's the difference between dating and living together. When you share the space day in and day out, certain things are going to emerge. (Good thing to talk about when you're doing pre-marital counseling!)

There's no way you can predict what such surprises may be. Of course, the parish profile and most of the people you meet during the interview process like the church the way it is. They are, after all, in leadership positions. They have some stake in the status quo.

When I was interviewing with St. Matthew's, I was fortunate in the degree of honesty people expressed before I was chosen as rector. Some were quite open about such felt needs as making a greater mark in the community, not being so cut off from other local institutions; about the need to form a more positive relationship with our diocese; about some financial difficulties that needed to be overcome.

It never occurred to me to ask, "What are your problems?" I was too eager to be called.

But once I was in place, the issues began to emerge. Within the first month several parishioners made appointments to see me, and each shared an egregious story about a fellow parishioner. Each was prefaced with the words: "Here's something you need to be aware of."

What should you do in such a situation? I'd suggest listening politely, thanking the person, and otherwise let the interview run its course.

You're still too new to know if the person is telling you the truth of if he or she has some personal axe to grind. It's going to take time. If it's a real problem, it will likely in time come to you from another source or sources. If not, it may go away and never surface again.

In my case, two of the issues were proven true. Both were verified in varieties of ways. One I dealt with in my third year as rector. The other finally came to a head after I left.

My best advice: listen, wait, and keep your antennae out for any functional or outstanding interpersonal irregularities.

Another issue had to do with something positive. It would be a dream come true for any church. What I'm talking about is a major bequest that came our way just a few months before I became rector. But the gift brought with it some difficulties none of us could have predicted.

A woman had died without heirs and left her considerable estate to St. Matthew's. It consisted of a large cash amount plus thirty-plus acres with a large manor house and four rental cottages. The woman's will didn't clearly specify how she wanted the church to use her gift.

The ultimate responsibility for how to read and interpret the will and subsequently how to use the gift was up to the vestry, who by Episcopal Canon Law has responsibility for church finances and properties. However, while I was still being interviewed, members of the search committee and vestry began asking me what I thought we should do with the bequest.

They were obviously looking to me for leadership. What now? Again— wait; don't do anything major for a year. I knew exactly what I thought should be done with the gift. Still, I waited a year.

Why wait on this one? Because I wanted to get to know the church well enough to choose logical members of a committee I then formed to study the will and make recommendations to the vestry.

When the year was up, I knew who should serve on the committee. I chose the chair. The wardens and I determined the committee members. We met. We hashed it over. We took plenty of time. We considered a variety of different ways of handling the properties and the money. We researched the possibilities of turning the place into a diocesan retreat center, converting it into a home for retired clergy or fixing up the houses and continuing to rent them. After some truly fraught times—particularly having to do with the rental properties and their tenants—the committee, vestry, and I came to the same decision. Which was: sell the property, pool the proceeds with the cash gift, invest it, and give an annual amount of cash to help struggling churches in our diocese and occasional other deserving causes. We also agreed the fund could be used for exceptional needs of our own church.

Once the decision was made, I was relieved to have it dealt with at last. One elderly tenant appeared on the front page of the local newspaper under a headline something like "Wealthy Church Evicts Needy Woman." Another local pastor read the paper, picked up the phone and called to tell me that because I was kicking out the tenants I was, in fact, not a Christian.

What he didn't know, because the article avoided mentioning it, was that we'd worked hard trying to find the woman a new place to live, which the church would pay for. She was finally placed, with the help of her daughter, in a retirement home.

There were also complaints from among our own. Several parishioners thought the money should all be used to help our church. A logical response, had we not had the financial wherewithal to fund our budget and raise special capital for building projects. Which we did.

One elderly lady, a great favorite of mine, had me to tea and told me that because of their decision to give the money away, I should fire the entire vestry and start over with candidates of her choice. I told her I couldn't do that. She said yes I could; as the rector I could do anything. I managed to avoid telling her that I was in total agreement with the vestry. We parted friends, but she never backed down.

Expect that. Some people are never going to be happy with some decisions. But in my experience as rector such stubborn resistance happened rarely. We were fortunate to maintain a happy agreement on virtually every major change and decision we made.

So we pressed on with our decision regarding the bequest, and the resultant committee we formed to entertain requests and determine recipients has managed the gift beautifully through the years. A lot of parishes and other worthwhile organizations have been helped.

The moral of this story is that you'll have surprises along the way. When they come, pray for wisdom, try not to let your emotions keep you from a clear-headed response and—finally—never be surprised by the surprises. They keep coming.

QUESTION 13

SHOULD I FOCUS ONLY ON AREAS OF PARISH LIFE THAT INTEREST ME?

IT DEPENDS ON THE SIZE OF YOUR PARISH

In corporate and large-program sized churches, you can't possibly focus on every ministry and activity. You'll need adequate numbers of staff, clergy and lay, with the gifts and interests to match the needs. As leader, you'll need to be aware of what's happening, without being unnecessarily burdened with nuts and bolts detail.

In a small church, you'll likely have some part in everything. Some of us prefer that, want to be involved with every aspect of parish life. Others of us know we're only going to be most effective when we stick to the tasks that help energize us.

Hopefully, we'll be able to pursue the aspects of ministry that delight us most.

Again, check out the expectations. When you're interviewing, it's good to ask what areas of ministry the rector traditionally covers. By Episcopal Church Canon Law, the rector's responsibilities are the spiritual life of the parish, including liturgies; all the events; staff; and chairing the vestry meetings.

Having said that, the church you come to may have traditions and expectations of "what the rector does." Some of these things are taken for granted. Some you only know about after you've failed to meet the expectations. Lord, grant us all the advance knowledge we can get!

QUESTION 14

I FEEL LONELY. I'M AFRAID IT MAY ADVERSELY AFFECT MY MINISTRY. WHAT SHOULD I DO?

FIGURE OUT WHY YOU'RE LONELY AND ADDRESS IT ASAP

Our lives as clergy can be isolating. Expectations are high. We're supposed to be all things to all people. It never occurs to some parishioners that we have real lives. Very few have any idea what our responsibilities consist of.

One man in his sixties had been a church-goer his entire life. Then his wife took a job as a bookkeeper in the parish office. After a few weeks, he came to me and said, "I'm embarrassed to admit this, but I always thought clergy mostly took off during the week and showed up for Sundays, baptisms, weddings, and funerals. I had *no idea* of the administrative and pastoral work it takes to be a rector."

I've been blessed to serve multi-staff churches. Which means I've always had colleagues to share thoughts, ideas, and impressions.

If you're the lone clergy in a small church in a small-town or country setting, you'll have to work overtime finding colleagues, friends, people to help offset the enforced isolation.

Whatever size church you serve, find ways to make friends. It can be hard for us to find the time to make friends aside from our parishioners. And parishioners *can* become friends. But we have to remember we're always their rector. Some things we shouldn't feel free to say or do because, though friends, we represent the Lord.

It can be a good idea to find a therapist you trust. Therapy can help you delve into, talk out, and through, issues and feelings that can contribute to your isolation and loneliness.

PART 2

LEADERSHIP

HOW CAN I BECOME A BETTER LEADER?

LEADERSHIP IS A GIFT THAT CAN BE DEVELOPED OR EVEN LEARNED

Leadership obsessed me when I first became a rector. How do you lead a parish?

Some people have the natural gift of leadership, but not all. Even if you don't, you can *learn* leadership techniques.

Never having taken a class or read a book on leadership, when I became rector, I started studying leadership. I read books, went back in my mind and thought about the leadership styles of people I'd understudied in my several careers.

If you haven't read Ed Friedman's book *Generation to Generation*, I recommend you do. In this book and when I heard him teach in person, he made clear these four suggestions for how to be an effective leader. They have undergirded my ministry.

HERE THEY ARE: UNDER-REACT; DEFINE YOURSELF; STAY ENGAGED; KEEP THE LIGHT TOUCH

Under-react

This one didn't come naturally to me. As a young man I was over- not under-reactive: flashfire temper, self-defensive, quick to absorb any tension in the room. But with time, even before I went to seminary, I cooled down. The Lord helped me. He'll help you, if you have some similar traits. Ask God for his help.

And when it comes to ministry, I agree with Dr. Friedman: When all around are tense with anxiety or animosity, even losing their tempers, as the leader you need to work overtime to stay calm. If the leader becomes as angry or anxious as everyone else, the negative emotions escalate and the group gets stuck in the problem. But if you stay relaxed, show them you're not freaking out, act as though it's all going to be okay (whether you're sure it is or not), the whole system relaxes and—even it if takes time—is able to move on to a creative solution.

Sometimes under-reacting means knowing when to call time out. I remember giving my daughters "time outs" when they were little. Time out meant going to your room for a while—to hopefully calm down, gain some perspective, removed from the heat of the moment.

I remember as rector tabling certain initiatives because members of the vestry were unable to agree to a solution in the moment. I could feel the tension rising, disagreement getting a little heated. Tabling carries with it the hope that by another meeting, people will have come to a more amicable solution. Sometimes it will mean forming a group to study the proposal and come up with more information that helps unify the group.

I did this rarely in my years as rector. Mostly, we had healthy discussion and debate—with virtually never even heated discussions, let alone anger. You may not be as fortunate. Whatever the situation, under-reacting is a valuable tool.

Define yourself

This means you need to be clear about where you stand. Always. The psychological term is "differentiation."

What's that? Among other things, *clarity*. Always make yourself clear, on every issue, on every decision you make. Give your reasons for why you do what you do. People may disagree with you, but at least they'll know where you stand—and why.

A poorly defined leader fosters anxiety in the system. You may come across as weak to some, which can lead to jockeying for power, among the laity or even members of your staff.

On the other hand, ask others for their opinion. They'll feel respected and valued and, whether you take their advice or not, be more willing to go with the choice you ultimately make.

Don't be afraid to say, "I don't know. I'm not sure." Be willing to ask for help. We're never going to know everything. We need to be open to continual taking in information and learning and listening—to the people around us and to the Lord . . . while all the time realizing the buck stops finally with us. A sometimes lonely place to be, it's also the one we've been called to and we're never completely alone. The Lord has our back!

Don't be heavy-handed; never aggressive or harsh. But if you're clear about where the church needs to be going, and how individual decisions and initiatives contribute to the overarching goals and visions, and if you adequately articulate your position, people tend to feel good about their place in the system. There's a lot less anxiety, stress, and tension. It's called health. And, above all, we need to be building healthy churches. Church growth may be an indication of health. But health should be your primary, underlying goal.

Stay engaged

I don't mean this negatively, but here's a way our parishioners can be like children. Like children, they know more about us than we think they do. They pick up things we may not think they're aware of. Sometimes, they see things in us we don't know are there ourselves.

For example, if you're feeling exhausted, a little bored, bordering on burn out, some of your people probably know it.

We're human. Why can't we feel these things? We can, of course. What we don't ever want the members of our church to feel is that we're bored or tired of being their pastor or leader. If we lose our interest in caring for them, if we lose our energy and excitement about leading their church, we need to get away and work on it.

Maybe you need spiritual direction, therapy, a vacation, membership in a workout club. Most of us know what it takes to rejuvenate us. Find a way to do it.

We must never, never let our people feel we don't care—for them or for the church.

We need to show them ways in which we care about them, their contributions, their families, their lives away from church. We're supposed to care—for them and about them. Because above all, the Lord cares.

All our ministries are different, as we're different. One thing has to be constant: we have to stay engaged with the people.

When they know we love them, they'll open themselves up to us as pastor, spiritual leader, and friend.

They'll trust us. And trust is the foundation of every relationship. If you don't have trust in a friendship, you don't have a friendship, you have an acquaintance. If you don't have trust in a marriage, you don't have a marriage, you have a contract. If you don't have trust between clergy and laity, you don't have the powerful relationships God needs to build his church.

Keep the light touch

George Bernard Shaw would have agreed. He said: "He who laughs lasts." It's true—true in marriage, true in parenting, true in friendship, true in ministry. In meetings, I always keep a look out for the opportunity to introduce levity. Not too often. Not too silly. Never by being flip, caustic, or even faintly off color. But be ready to inject, hopefully, just the right amount of humor. Even a touch of humor, introduced in the right way at the right moment, can keep a meeting from hardening into a logjam of irreconcilable differences.

Try humor when you can. It's both reconciling and unifying.

"Laughter is social," says neuroscientist Robert R. Provine, an emeritus professor of psychology at the University of Maryland, Baltimore County. "It's about relationships. Laughter is a social activity that allows people to communicate and to deepen alliances and friendships." ("The Science of Laughter: Our Bodies. Our Minds. Our Souls." Special *Time Magazine* edition, 2018.)

More than once I've used humor to save a meeting from shipwreck. It may even save your ministry.

Most important, when we can laugh—at a situation and especially at ourselves—we're reminding ourselves and everyone else that the Lord is in control, that we don't have to carry it by ourselves, that by faith we trust he's going to bring us through to victory.

When you're in the trenches and fire's raining down on you, laughter becomes the ultimate faith assertion. And as the leader, being able to laugh in a tight situation is as important as being able to say I was wrong.

Who says it better than G. K. Chesterton? "Angels can fly because they take themselves lightly."

One more aspect of our clergy leadership is our visibility. We're upfront at virtually every service. Polls show that our preaching—and our personality—can draw people or drive them away. If we're doing our job, we're up in front communicating positively, out in front leading the way. As someone said about sports: "Sports don't build character, they reveal it."

The same can be said of the leadership we do. (Edwin H. Friedman, *Generation to Generation: Family Process in Church and Synagogue*. London: The Guilford Press, 1985).

QUESTION 16

WHAT'S THE KEY
TO CHURCH LEADERSHIP?

I HAVE ONE ANSWER: REMEMBER YOU ARE CALLED

Nothing has helped me stay grounded, centered, and focused in ministry more than remembering that *God has called me to this.*

Martin Luther could be heard walking through the streets on rainy days chanting: "Remember your baptism. Remember your baptism. Remember your baptism."

We have to remember our call.

God has either called you to ministry or he hasn't. There's no such thing as a self-call. People have said to me through the years, "When did you decide to be a minister?"

The answer is, I didn't decide. I answered a call. I remember as a little boy hearing some distant cousin had been "called to the ministry." I remember wondering, even at that early age, "What's a call?" I asked my mother. She said, "Its means God wants you to do a special work for him."

"But how does it happen? What does it look like?" I asked, but she had no answers. People still ask me how a call works, what it feels like. To which I can only say you know when you have it. You know that you know that you know. You know that you have to be ordained. It's when you know you can't *not* do it. It's like marrying the right person for you—you feel you can't live without that person. Any other reason to get married is too weak a connection to guarantee the long haul. The same is true of ministry.

I've seen too many ministers ship-wrecked because they made a decision rather than answered a call. I'm not proud to admit it, but I resisted the Lord's call for three years. I didn't want to be ordained. It wasn't my idea. It was the Lord's. Like Moses, I argued. Like the unbelieving Greeks, I asked him to give me signs. Which he did—miraculously, one after another, each one more dramatic than the one before—until I was forced to give up, cry "Uncle," and go to seminary. But once there, I never questioned my call again. By then, I knew that I knew.

He calls us because he has a particular work to do through us, by his Spirit. As he has called us out of darkness into light, so he calls us out of our former lives as lay people into the vocation of the ordained.

It's a call to *service*. Service to him, to his people, to the church, and to the world.

It's a love call, a passionate love call. Church growth expert Lyle Schaller said, "The difference between a job and ministry is one word: passion."

For love, passionate love, the bride in the Song of Solomon learns how she can spend every day with her bridegroom. It's by going where he goes, helping him tend his sheep.

For love, Peter, hearing Jesus' call to him from the beach, leaps out of the boat of his old career and old life into the water and onto the beach of a new career, a new vocation, a new life. "Peter, if you love me, tend my sheep."

It's for love that we do what we do—as the called, the chosen, the ordained of God. It's the holy call of a holy God to minister his holy word and sacraments and mercy to his holy people.

For people like us, there is no greater joy!

QUESTION 17

WHAT TRAITS SHOULD
A CLERGY LEADER CULTIVATE?

THE THREE E'S OF PARISH LEADERSHIP:
ENERGY; ENTHUSIASM; ENJOYMENT

You may think, "These don't sound like very godly characteristics. I'd think things like prayer, preaching, compassion, and a love of the sacraments are more important." And so they are, in a way. But those are all things we *do*. What I'm talking about here is how we *are* as leaders; about the approach and attitude we bring to our work for the Lord.

Energy and Enthusiasm

Energy and enthusiasm are closely, even inextricably, linked. I can't see one without the other when it comes to ministry.

Both are crucial approaches for us to bring to leading worship, preaching and teaching, chairing meetings, and interacting with our parishioners.

There are days when it's a low Sunday (the first Sunday after Christmas and Easter; vacation times). Turnout is rock bottom. Or maybe a lot of your people were up late the night before at a major town or neighborhood function. Or the weather's lousy. Or it's simply a dull, gray, bleak day. All it takes is low barometric pressure to deep-six the energy.

On mornings like this, it all depends on us. It depends on the leader. There's nothing worse than a dispirited worship service. It's an oxymoron. Worship is an encounter with the divine. Worship is our reminder that the living God is with us—according to his promise: "Wherever two or three are gathered together in my name, there I am in the midst of you." When the Lord is manifestly present in the sanctuary of his people, he brings with him joy, energy, life. We should by rights take our shoes off when we come into church because, like Moses, we are on holy ground. Because God is with us. We are in The Presence. The bush burns!

When we as leaders forget the awesomeness of these holy moments, how can we expect the people to remember? We may be fortunate enough to have some in the pews who are sufficiently spiritually connected, who totally get it, who are here prepared to lay themselves heart and soul before the Lord in worship. But we can't depend on it. And it's not their responsibility to carry and convey the light, it's ours.

How many services have you been to that were dull, draggy, and—worst of all—boring?

On mornings when everything and everybody seems down, it's up to me. I force myself, however dull and dispirited I may also feel, to be upbeat. This is no time for my personal feelings. As always, it's not about me, it's about God and his people. I "whump it up."

On days like this, in the prayer time just before we go in, I tell the choir and others involved in the service that it's up to us to make it happen. Sometimes on a down morning I say, "Okay, folks, it's a punch-through morning. Let's do it!"

Punch-through? When I was a kid growing up in the Midwest, the high school football teams would run onto the field in single line. The first boy charged through a big metal circle covered with the team insignia printed on a piece of butcher paper. He literally punched through the paper to lead his team onto the field. Sometimes you and I have to lead our worship team and everyone else in church in punching through to a place of joy and expectancy in worship.

We've all seen worship leaders, preachers, and teachers who are low energy, who come across as tired, bored, or both. For us, it must never be. We are handling the things of God. As preachers, we are submitting ourselves to his Spirit to enable us to preach his word. There is nothing boring about God, about his word, about what his Spirit wants to do in us and through us. As teachers, we're answering another call—to break the bread of life, God's Word, in such a way that it's always fresh bread. Nobody wants stale bread.

If you're tired, ask him to energize you. If you're bored, consider your call, the possibility of burnout. Beg him to renew and revive you. If you lack passion, come back to him and pray for an infusion of his Spirit, for a manifestation of himself that will restore you to your first love.

Sundays are when you see the greatest percentage of your congregation on a regular basis. Give them everything you've got and, if possible, don't plan too much for Sunday afternoon. I'd usually run by the hospital if someone was in crisis, then home for time with my family and, ideally, a nap! Five o'clock service? I've been fortunate to serve in multi-clergy situations, so we took turns.

Energy and enthusiasm also apply to every meeting we chair or attend. As leaders, we set the tone for the entire parish.

Energy and enthusiasm are important in how we interact with our parishioners. Never, never, never come across as bored or disinterested. When you see a parishioner, that person is the most important person in the world to you at that moment.

A man once sat at dinner between two famous and talented women— each renowned in her career. At the end of the evening, his wife asked him: "What was it like sitting between two such powerful and accomplished women?" The husband answered, "When dinner was over, I was convinced Lady A was the most charming and interesting person in the room. When dinner was over, Lady B had made me feel I was the most charming and interesting person in the room."

Interchanges between you and your people are never about you. They are always about them.

I'm reminded of what a member of the English royal family once said: "We are never tired. We are never bored. And we love hospitals." Same with us.

No matter how boring or complaining or whining a parishioner may seem to you in the moment, standing before you is God's cherished creation. He gave his life for this person. The person pouring his or her heart out to you or simply droning on and on at coffee hour about what seems the most mundane things, deserves your *total* attention. Don't look around the room to see who else is there, don't even look for newcomers. That's why you have a member of your Welcome Committee assigned to every coffee hour.

Keep your eyes, keep all your attention, focused on the person in front of you. And when you finally are able to break away, do it gently. You are that person's pastor, and your call is to minister with equal devotion to the seemingly less lovable as well as to the more obviously lovable.

Years ago, when I was in a prayer group in Atlanta, we had a young woman, Claudia, who ostensibly had little going for her. Drastically over-weight, slightly mentally challenged, she was the one who always asked for prayer. Her craving for attention was obvious and, frankly, annoying.

I complained once about the young woman to a leader of the group, an older woman, Myra.

In response to my complaint, instead of agreeing with me, Myra chuckled. "But, Terry," Myra said, "don't you see? The Lord has given you Claudia as a rubbing stone. Claudia has the ministry of the rubbing stone to our group. When certain rough edges have been rubbed away, she won't bug us quite so much. And we will shine as gold!"

You'll always have some rubbing stones. Ask the Lord to help you love them. Ask him to show you what in you needs to be rubbed away.

And when you're really having a hard time with someone particularly needy and/or clingy remember Paul: "The members of the body that seem to be weaker are indispensable, and those members of the body that we think less honorable are clothed with greater honor" (1 Corinthians 12:24).

Enjoyment

Here's another royalty story. On the day the British nation was celebrating the one hundredth birthday of Queen Elizabeth the Queen Mother with a joyous parade in London, someone turned to the old lady standing, not sitting, on the reviewing stand and remarked how wonderful it was that she seemed to be having such a good time. But shouldn't she sit? The queen said, "There's no point in being a hundred if you can't enjoy yourself."

Two other centenarians, two of the great entertainers of the last centu-ry, Bob Hope and George Burns, also made it to a hundred. Is it surprising that these two men spent their long careers making people laugh—and no doubt getting enjoyment from giving enjoyment through so many years?

Faith—the noun—can be taught. Active faith, owned faith, lived faith—faith as verb—can't be taught. It must be *caught*. When our faith is dynamic, radiant, alive, it becomes contagious to other people. We carry with us a spirit of enjoyment. We are living the abundant life. We are walk-ing in the joy of the Lord. We see, in him, each day as a new opportunity. Cranky, depressed, down at the mouth clergy don't infect anybody with the light of Christ.

Of course, there are the down times, the discouraging times, the frustrating times, even the tragic times. That's another story. Our goal then is to be appropriate, as best we can, for the people we're ministering to.

Mostly, though, the closer we walk with God, the more we ask and allow him to fill us with his Spirit, the more we will enjoy life and our ministry.

Look for ways to enjoy life, to make the most of every day. The same rector who told me we shouldn't complain to our people also tended to turn cranky when feeling overwhelmed. As his associate, I wrote these words on a three-by-five card: HAVE FUN. When he was having a bad day, I would walk in and lay the card on his desk. It happened a lot; and it worked every time. He looked at the card and laughed. One time he came in and laid a card with HAVE FUN on my desk. Works both ways.

The high point of my week—the moment I enjoyed most as rector— was when I stood in the side door of the church, the procession formed and ready to go into worship, and watched the people coming down the driveway from the parking lot to church. The saints of God hurrying to worship him. What could be better?

Happiness depends on the happenings, the events, and relationships in our lives going well. Joy is not dependent on happenstance. Joy springs from our relationship with God—and it's contagious. So are your and my energy, enthusiasm, and enjoyment.

"The joy of the LORD is our strength."

QUESTION 18

HOW CAN I JUGGLE SO MANY DEMANDS?

YOU HAVE TO BE ABLE TO MAKE QUICK SHIFTS

Fortunately for me, I have a mild case of ADHD. I was diagnosed in late middle age. When I say "fortunately" I'm only half joking, because despite the drawbacks, I've found plusses in the condition. As a rector my natural inclination to do a whole lot of different things at virtually the same time has proved helpful.

I admire the clergy I know who have intense power of concentration. For them, focus comes naturally. I have to work hard to focus for any but brief spells. However, my natural "quick shift" mind set enables me to live into something my most important ministry mentor—Washington, DC, rector, John Harper—once told me. He said, "To be a parish priest is to be the last true generalist in the culture. You have to be prepared every day to keep changing course. From meeting with staff to visiting someone in the hospital. To planning a baptism or doing pre-marital counseling to holding the hand of a beloved parishioner who's desperately ill or dying. You're always shifting from one thing to another."

John was, of course, right. Consider some of the varied skills we're expected to possess: Preach and teach. Manage employees. Identify and encourage lay leaders. Know how to read and comprehend budgets. Connect with parishioners of every age. Design and execute and lead liturgies appropriate to seasonal or pastoral requirements. Articulate the vision for the parish. Manage conflict. Inspire your parishioners to care for each other and for the needy outside your doors. Be with people at their most intimate times of joy and sorrow.

There are more. With time, you'll add your own. But the main thing is to expect the unexpected and not be surprised when it happens.

BE FLEXIBLE

Like a successful prize-fighter, as church leaders we need to stay light on our feet, always expecting the next—if not blow—surprise. When a blow connects, we need to do our best to deflect it: yes, turn the cheek, try hard not to take it personally, go the Lord for help, and keep our sense of humor if we possibly can.

My dad used to say with his colloquial Midwestern turn of phrase, "If you can't laugh, you're a goner." We must refuse to be goners. We signed on for the long haul. We've been ordained for life.

Years ago, I asked a retired bishop's wife how she and her husband of many years had handled the vagaries of marriage and pastoral life.

She said, "I adapted the habit of always trying to see the absurdity in any situation. Invariably it took me out of myself and made me laugh. Sometimes I was the most absurd of all! The reason I know God has a sense of humor is because he made me."

That's one of the reasons I always get to church services thirty minutes early, because I want to be prepared for something unexpected. Such as, some key person not showing up or, as happened one blustery winter morning, discovering that the heating had gone off in the middle of the night.

WHAT ARE RECURRING THEMES IN CHURCH LEADERSHIP?

TEN THEMES OF MINISTRY IN THE LOCAL CHURCH

1. Be prepared to work hard

Get ready. Leading a church is not like other jobs. Partly because it's not a job—though on your bad days, it may feel like one—it's a call.

As in marriage, you're not married only when you feel like it or when you're not tired or feeling down. And when you're parenting a little child, that child doesn't keep you awake at night because you didn't really need that night's sleep. So it is with ministry.

2. Take your day off, but stay reachable/connected

As indicated earlier, my day-off was Friday. Why Friday? Though most clergy seem to take Mondays off, I found that in the parishes I've served, my parishioners are back at work, starting up their week, turning to business at hand, which for some of them some of the time meant contacting me. I'd rather be there to deal with their questions and concerns than get to them a day later.

I remember one of my assistants asking me how many units he was expected to work per week. I think he learned the term "units" in seminary. I've never thought of my ministry in units, but more as a continuum. As in, I'm always the rector. One thing that means is that though I obviously have to take time away and get vacations, I'm always connected.

I've always told my staff, clergy and lay, and my wardens that wherever I may be—on whatever break, even if I'm out of the country—they must contact me with a major question or dilemma. I'd much rather take the time out to help them manage their problem than to have them suffer alone or through lack of experience make a potentially less-than-ideal decision. Sometimes they'll feel better just talking it through with you.

Then there are the parishioners who don't want to feel you're out of touch. I've been fortunate, my parishioners virtually never contacted me when I was on a study break or vacation.

There was the time, though, when I came back from a week at Oxford. A parishioner who'd been quite ill, said, "I tried to reach you and couldn't." That was in the early days of cell phone service, and I hadn't even taken my phone with me. The next time I left the country, my phone went with me.

3. Make the most of every day

I love to work out. But I learned to do double duty on the elliptical machine: while accruing the miles and breaking a sweat, I'm always reading some ministry-related book. You might rather do it via headphones.

We all know what re-charges us. We need to factor those helps into the days and weeks of our lives. Jesus took time away. So must we. We don't prove anything by burning ourselves out. That said, there will be times when circumstances over which you really don't have control bring you to the point of exhaustion. When that happens, do everything you can to balance it with away time with the Lord.

"He that dwelleth in the secret place of the Most High abides in the shadow of the Almighty," we know from reading Psalm 91. Those times apart in the secret place can be the most important, even essential and sometimes crucial, times for as leaders. It's in those times of spirit renewing, creativity enhancing, mentally uplifting moments with him that we get what we need to keep doing the work he's called us to.

4. Persevere

We all know the importance of perseverance. In my lifetime it's become a pop culture term. That was not true in my growing up years; partly because as the son of Great Depression/World War II parents, perseverance was taken for granted. You persevered and survived (for my family) the shattering hardship of farm-belt economic depression. You persevered and did your part to help win the war and save democracy.

Now sometimes the virtue of persistence has to be taught. Simply put, you won't last long as chief pastor without it. And without a persevering leader the church won't go where the Lord wants it to go or accomplish the goals he has in mind for it.

5. Learn the history; tell the story

It pays to be curious about the church you've just come to. If you're the leader, you need to care enough about the place, its people—past and present and how it got to where it is today—to be not only the chief encourager but also the chief booster.

If you can't love that church, maybe you shouldn't have accepted the call. Show the people you're interested in every aspect of the life they've shared through the years.

Learn the stories. Seek them out. Remember them. Learn the oral tradition. Keep it alive for the children growing up under your leadership. I think of the marvelous old Irish tradition of the storyteller, men who used to wander from town to town telling stories.

The storyteller would simply show up in someone's house. He'd be greeted with open arms; given food and lodging for however long he chose to stay. The word would go out: "The storyteller's at the O'Malley's!"

And every night for as long as he stayed, the O'Malley's house would be crammed with people of all ages listening—rapt, enchanted—to the stories he magically wove. They were stories of their land, their people, their history. Stories that affirmed their identity as individuals and as a people. The storyteller helped remind people who they were, what they stood for, where they'd been, why they were where they were now, and where they might be going.

So must you be a storyteller: telling the stories of our Lord—both from your own and other's experiences and from his word, telling the stories of the church he has brought you to serve.

Every Sunday is a story moment. We remind ourselves what it means to be the people of God, standing on the shoulders, building on the work of our spiritual ancestors. We remind ourselves that we are charged as his people today to go forth and—empowered by his Spirit—change the world for him.

Always remember—as chief pastor you're not only the chief encourager and prime motivator, you're also the keeper of the Flame.

6. Be willing to try

My children hated it, but from time to time during their growing up years, I'd trot it out, the old saw: "Learn anything?"

One of my daughters actually came to me a few years ago and said, "Dad, I sure didn't like it at the time. But when I messed up and you asked me that question, when I got over being defensive, I usually would think about what you said. And usually I actually learned something from what I'd done. If only not to do it again!"

There are times when we have to swallow our ego (I don't know about you, but not always easy for me), and admit we made a mistake.

Another of my dad's sayings was, "Do something, even if it's wrong."

I've applied that to being willing to try anything. Be prepared, however, for those parishioners who don't want that change you're proposing.

I was confronted with that mindset in some parishioners shortly after I arrived as rector. In one of my first vestry meetings I told the vestry, "If you think in me you've called a maintenance man, I've given the wrong impression. I'm a *mission* man. We're going to move out and do new things for God."

I started by saying we needed to grow—spiritually and in numbers. And, I said, we needed to tend to buildings too long neglected. We needed to both repair and restore but also add on to some of our existing structures, a reflection of the other ways we were growing.

The need to fund and oversee building programs was one of my surprises as a new rector. I'd never thought of myself as a buildings and grounds specialist. But you do what's needed.

A few people put up some resistance. But not many, and not much. The case was so clearly made for building restoration and expansion, we launched a successful capital campaign less than two years after I arrived. And when the projects were completed, some of the proudest proponents of the finished products had been some of the most vocal initial naysayers.

7. Expect both successes and failures

Though I've always emphasized health over numbers and never growth for growth sake, you still need to be consistently trying to increase membership.

When they heard me say this, some people said they weren't interested in drawing new parishioners. To them I explained that no church stays the same. People get transferred. They retire and move to a more congenial climate. Or they go to be with the Lord. If you don't add numbers, you'll die.

Fortunately, the majority agreed. We began to build. And we were successful—with God's help in ways that exceeded my dreams.

(Note: back to my earlier comment about not changing anything major early in your ministry. I certainly did not. And I valued the so-called "icon" traditions for all the twenty-three years I was rector.)

People are astonished when I tell them that in all those years we never had any major conflicts. But it's true. That's not to say we never had our ups and downs. Or mistakes. Or that I didn't sometimes wish I hadn't done something I did.

I've always had the theory that a busy church is a happy church. If parishioners feel their church is busy, energetically doing the work of the Lord; if they know and buy into the vision and goals, they both feel good about their church and, usually, they feel good about you, their leader. The number of programs, including new programs, depends, of course, on the number of congregants and their time, abilities, and financial wherewithal.

You have to be astute in determining how much is too much.

We launched a lot of new initiatives in my years as rector. Every time, I tested the waters, made sure I had the right people and the right number of people on board to carry them through.

My one major blunder was not entirely of my doing, though I have to take some responsibility. I had the idea of a sister parish relationship with a church in a very different socioeconomic community from ours. My dream was for joint projects with our youth groups, shared outreach projects, and social get-togethers. We had some positive experiences together, but the project never really took off.

My advance team and I had done a lot of planning but in retrospect not sufficient homework to anticipate potential pitfalls. Fortunately, we recovered with no one on either side angry or disaffected.

In retrospect, I came up with this list:

- Was our rationale sound?

- Did we do sufficient research?

- How and why did we fail?

- What did we manage to salvage? What were the positives in the experience? There were several.

7. What did we learn?

Everything is a learning experience. That's why we never give up, never quit trying, never quit asking the Lord to show us what's next.

Churches in order to stay alive, need to keep moving forward, need to be willing to experiment, adapt to the changing world, experiment with new ways of being church. We have to bravely keep trying new things. Be open to the possibility of failure. Even when it hurts. And it will hurt.

8. Stay relevant

I'm convinced we're *not* being called to adapt to all the changes of the world. Websites, podcasts, online stewardship opportunities, including parishioner's cell-phone numbers and email addresses (if they approve) in your church directory—yes. But part of what it means to be the church is that we don't take in everything the world approves of.

I'm not one of Richard Neibuhr identifies, in his landmark typologies, as a "Christ *of* culture" man. (Richard Niebuhr, *Christ and Culture*, New York: Harper, 1951.) We need to be *in* the culture, but not always *of* the culture. We need to remember we're kingdom people. We need to show a higher way, preach and teach and model a kingdom viewpoint. We need to be, again in Niebuhr's understanding, *"transformers* of culture."

Part of our tradition of continuity (even repetition), maintaining our beliefs, values, and forms of worship are what make the church a haven, a safe place for so many of our people who sometimes need refuge from a world that can feel overwhelming, scary, and confusing.

On the other hand, there can be a fine point between continuity and boredom. How many children have you heard say, "I don't like church. Church is boring." Sadly, all too often, they're right—not just for them, but for the adults, too.

We can't turn ourselves into slaves of the culture trying to be relevant. Still, we know the only constant is change. My challenge has always been: how do we change enough to be able to speak to where people are in their lives and in the world, while being true to God's call as his church? This is the challenge of a lifetime. Which brings me to the fifth recurring theme:

9. Learn to love challenge more than comfort

Every leader, to be effective, has to learn and live this truism. When God called us, he didn't call us to lives of comfort.

A lot about my life as rector was comfortable, nurturing, and affirming. But certainly not all. And if I began to feel a little too comfortable, I told myself to look around and see where we needed change, improvement, or, as a New Hampshire friend of mine said, "tweaking."

Some program getting a little stale? Liturgies need a little work? What about a new church school curriculum? Are we doing the best we can do at integrating new members? Doing all we can in outreach? (The answer to that was usually, no.) We all have our list.

One reason we can't preach comfort with the culture, is because too much of the world lives counter to the gospel. But, personally, we can't let ourselves get comfortable with our own personal status quo, either.

Though God loves us just as we are, he doesn't want us to stay that way. His goal for us is to grow increasingly more like Jesus. If I'm going to become the image and likeness of Jesus; if, in the apostle Paul's words, all of us Christians are to become what he calls "the fragrance of Christ," we have work to do. That means me as well as my parishioners.

Writes Paul:

> But thanks be to God, who always leads us in his triumph in Christ, and manifests through us the sweet aroma of the knowledge of him in every place. For we are a fragrance of Christ to God among those who are perishing, to the one an aroma from death to death, to the other an aroma from life to life.
> (2 Corinthians 2:14–16)

I can't speak for you, but there are days when I smell a whole lot more like Old Spice than I do the Spirit of God. But I don't stop trying.

Comfort is not the path the average Christian walks to be changed into the likeness of Christ. But if we're true to him and to his call, that's our goal. And, my fellow shepherds, not just for ourselves but also for our churches. As Christians and as leaders in the body of Christ, we must give ourselves over to the inner working of the Holy Spirit so that, again in the words of Paul, we may be "transformed into his image from glory to glory" (2 Corinthians 3:18)

10. Build

When you're leading a church, you need to be constantly building.

Build your own relationships with the people.

Build Christian community—which includes Bible studies, fellowship activities, small groups, and encouraging your people to care for each other.

Build good will in the greater community by reaching out in mission to the needy and inviting people beyond your doors to such events as concerts and lectures.

Build your and their relationship with the Lord. That's our chief purpose, of course, to lead them in worship and by worship, preaching, teaching, and example help guide them into the ineffable joys of ever-deepening relationship with him.

QUESTION 20

HOW DO I FORMULATE A VISION?

CONSIDER YOUR STRENGTHS AS A CHURCH

Visioning is an enormous responsibility. But the primary responsibility is yours.

"Without a vision the people perish," we're told in Proverbs 29:18. I know it's a cliché but like all clichés it's based on time-tested truth. To be a successful church, you need to know where you're going.

Just as in your first visioning retreat, you and your leadership need to keep remembering what your church does best. If you try too many things, if you move beyond your resources—not just financially, but socially and personally—you'll dilute your effect and weaken your mission.

What are those strengths? I built, and kept building, on those strengths with the congregation, encouraging their input and participation, reminding them of how fortunate we were to have these unique gifts from the Lord, gifts to us, gifts to our visitors and new members, gifts (some of them) to the greater community.

ASSESS AND REASSESS

Poll your lay leadership. At every annual retreat spend some time listening to where they feel the church is now. Be open to anything: successes, failures, personal reflections. How would they describe the church to an outsider? Be prepared to hear some personal gripes. These are the reasons I love this church. Which new initiatives do they feel have been successful—or not. Why? You may not learn much new or different from your first-year "boat ride," but it's important to give them this time. The church, like individuals, is always changing, always responding (or should be to some degree) to challenges in the culture and local community.

NOW WHAT?

Where does God want you to go next? Vision has to do with more than your church's existing strong points. From this foundation, where are you going? What new things does the Lord want you to take on? The Holy Spirit is God in action. He'll encourage us to take times out—as individual believers, as church leadership. But he doesn't want us stalled out. We need to go aside to pray and seek his guidance for the changes and new initiatives he wants us to take. As leaders we need to be willing to be the prime risk-takers. If we aren't willing to move out of our place of comfort and try something new, we can't expect it of our people.

ENCOURAGE WILLINGNESS TO MAKE CHANGES

Maybe you need to refine or even discontinue some or your programs. Take a fresh look at how you welcome visitors and incorporate new members. Are you initially friendly, welcoming? Are there any ways we may be un-knowingly turning off first timers? Is there some community outreach need we could or should be addressing? Maybe we need to take a fresh look at how we involve our teens—both in the church and in the world.

Our call to play a role alongside the Lord in shaping his church—in a certain community, in a given time in history—is a monumental respon-sibility. To have the trust in God and therefore the boldness to believe that he is actually both revealing things to you and using you to help realize his vision, can feel scary. It can also be tremendously exhilarating.

There were times when as rector I had to overcome the vestry's valid concerns and logical objections to major initiatives and assure them that what I felt was the right thing to do would actually work.

Your personal motivation is going to be tested. Repeatedly. Can you see it through? Do you have the resolve to press through strong resistance, to survive if you fail?

As chief visionary, you need to be willing to take responsibility for the disaster, should it occur.

ANTICIPATE

Part of visioning is anticipating what lies ahead. I used to tell my clergy associates that 80 percent of church leadership is anticipating. You have to be constantly anticipating how what you do is going to affect others.

I've known plenty of clergy who have come in and made arbitrary changes without testing the waters, without polling the troops, without considering how these changes might impact the people involved. As I pointed out earlier, this can be disastrous.

What we need to realize is that things are being done the way they're being done because somehow, even though it may not be how we'd do it, it's working for the people engaged in the endeavor. And probably been working for a long time.

For example, I knew a young clergy assistant, new to the church, who came in and began telling the altar guild how to do certain things with the setup of the altar that went counter to how they'd been done for some twenty years. Instead of telling them, he should have sat down with the head of the altar guild and others involved and told them he had some thoughts and what did they think about it.

Such an approach shows these long-time church volunteers that you value what they've been doing and how they've been doing it. It shows them you respect their contributions.

DON'T GO IT ALONE

Before you make any change get as many people as possible on board. The same thing is true of major changes and new initiatives. Introduce them widely and with as much rationale and eloquence as you can muster.

NEVER BE IN A HURRY

Above all, people want to be heard, need to feel their ideas and opinions matter. Take your time. Be patient. If people feel heard, they still may not agree with your decision, but at least they'll know you respected them enough to ask for their opinion and listen to it.

ASK QUESTIONS

Make sure you quiz your vestry or board, your committees and small groups. For changes that effect all the members, poll the entire church with an online questionnaire. Tell them what you've told them. People need to feel part of what's happening in their church. I've seen church leaders get into more trouble for making unilateral decisions than for any other thing.

Ask for feedback and be willing to take it, even when it's not what you expected—or wanted.

READ THE LOCAL CULTURE

You need to anticipate what may lie ahead in your local community. Are the demographics changing or staying the same? If your people are mostly communicating and doing a lot of their business online—which many are—make your church communications technologically savvy and computer friendly. Encourage online stewardship, for example.

A familiar member of any community in ancient times was the watchman. These were the men assigned to spend their days on top of a gate tower peering into the distance to see what might be coming. They learned to study the horizon and read what it might mean. A change in the weather. People coming your way—alone or in groups. It was up to the watchman to determine if those who were approaching might be friend or foe so the town could adjust accordingly. Sometimes he got it wrong, but usually— through wisdom gained from experience, he learned to gauge and appropriately respond to what was coming.

You and I are called to be cultural watchmen. Just as we need to try to make sense of what's happening now in the world around us, so we need to keep looking ahead, searching and studying the horizon. We need to be asking: If we're here now, if these things are taking place, where might it lead? How might it impact our people?

We must not be bound by trends and fads, by the tyranny of the popular and the immediate. Even the world of fashion understands that. Designer Karl Lagerfeld was quoted as saying, "What's trendy today will be tacky tomorrow."

To be relevant to our people's lives, to adequately address their problems, opportunities, and frustrations, to be sensitive to the current zeitgeist but not bound by it, that's some of the responsibility we take on when we begin the visioning process.

REMEMBER YOUR FOUNDATION

You and your lay leadership need to ask, who are we and why are we here? The timeless works of creativity have survived the ages because they plumbed the depths of universal human need and aspiration.

That's true for us as church leaders. If our new initiatives are to survive and flourish, they need to be based on the timeless principles of our tradition. You can't build lasting work for God if you don't build on his foundation. But when you do, what you build is going to last forever.

Some things never change—God's love for his people, the abiding themes of our common humanity. They must never be discarded. Look back and keep looking back to God's original idea of a people who will be *his* people.

Go to the Bible and you'll see his purpose hasn't changed since the beginning.

Turn to Exodus and hear Moses speaking the Lord's words to the children of Israel: "Now then, if you will indeed obey My voice and keep My covenant, then you shall be My own possession among all the peoples, for all the earth is Mine; and you shall be to Me a kingdom of priests and a holy nation" (Exodus 19:5-6).

Twelve hundred years later, Peter says to the new church: "But you are a chosen race, a royal priesthood, a holy nation, a people for God's own possession, that you may declare the wonderful deeds of him who has called you out of darkness into his marvelous light; for you once were not a people, but now you are the people of God" (1 Peter 2:9–10).

Twelve hundred years have passed, and God's purpose is still the same for the first Christians as it had been for the newly-forming nation and people of Israel. Two thousand-plus years later, the Lord has the same purpose for us today.

Now we are the royal priesthood. We are the holy nation. We are God's people called out of the world, drawn out of the darkness of sin and self-absorption and into the light of his love, forgiveness, and challenge so that we can show the world God—God in us, God shining forth out of us.

NEVER LOSE HEART

We know the church has changed, is continually changing, must change with the passing of time. We can find hope not despair in this, because God is with us. If we're going where he's taking us, the ride—though it can be difficult, even frightening—will also be exhilarating. As an old mentor of mine once said, "Walking with the Lord can be hard, but it's glorious!"

We shouldn't be shocked by the changes in the culture, drastic and sometimes deplorable though they may be to us. Because the Lord is fully able to help his church not only survive but even *thrive* in the midst of cataclysmic change.

DREAM BIG

Help the people dream big dreams. People get excited by big dreams. They want to support big dreams.

ALWAYS BE ON THE LOOKOUT FOR WHAT'S NEXT

We can be sure of something else: though the timeless principles hold, at the same time God is always doing a new thing. He's always communicating his will to us. Our responsibility is to listen, to hear, and to carry out his plan for us and for the people he trusts us to lead.

Just as Jesus said in one of his first post-resurrection appearances, "Tell them I am going on to Galilee," so we need to be willing to hear him say something we don't expect, something that may shake and even confound us.

DON'T LET FEAR GET IN THE WAY

Resist fear—fear of failure, fear that we might not be able to hear him, fear that we might not be up to the task of carrying out the plan he has in mind. We are not to fear his will—for us of for his church. He is with us. He will see his work to completion. He's on the road to Galilee, and he's calling us to come with him.

HOW DO WE DETERMINE PRIORITIES WHEN FUNDS ARE SCARCE?

REMEMBER THE BASICS

Whatever its size, every church is a community, cause, and corporation.

As leaders, we need to keep reminding people of why we're here.

As a worshipping community of Jesus' followers, we're called to reveal him to the world, continue his ministry to the lost and needy, and live in loving fellowship with our Lord and each other.

These are our responsibilities. They are also our opportunities. None need require a lot of money to carry out.

One of the sweetest examples of Christian community I've ever experienced met in the finished basement of a house in suburban Atlanta. No overhead. No pledges. But inspirational contemporary worship, excellent preaching and teaching, and a profound sense of connection with the Lord and with each other.

But for us denominational leaders, we have for one thing the responsibilities of property maintenance and upkeep. One of the drawbacks we may have are buildings and grounds that may require an outsize portion of our annual budget. Staff also tends to require a big outlay. These two budget items are necessary, but, depending on your financial capacity, they may leave little to support mission.

When that's the case, you need to look for ways to help address the outreach needs in your community without much expenditure. Encourage your people to volunteer at various charitable organizations. Reach out in other ways that meet the needs unique to your area. For example, we had a women's detention center near us. A good number of the women of our church found ways to connect with women in the prison. One launched and helped fund a ministry to children of parishioners.

Money is sometimes necessary to make the impact you want to make. But not always. Preach and teach a reaching-out mentality. Organize your people. Get creative about how to help others. Ask the Lord for fresh ideas. With his help, you can do great things for the needy ones of your community.

QUESTION 22

HOW DO I DO LONG-RANGE PLANNING?

When I'd been rector for fifteen years, I initiated a long-range planning process.

It was important for us to stand back, take stock, appraise where we'd been, what we'd accomplished, and also consider important initiatives for the future.

HOW DO YOU DO LONG-RANGE PLANNING?

Form a committee

Not too large, so you won't get bogged down with too many opinions. I chose our two wardens and two other vestry members, two former vestry members, and one at-large from the parish. Counting me that made eight. Eight seemed a good number—plus in Hebrew eight stands for new beginnings. Might as well be numerologically correct, right?

Number nine, the facilitator. Choose a strong facilitator—someone who is well-respected in the parish, has a calm demeanor, and has leadership ability. The facilitator is not considered a part of the committee—which emphasizes his or her role as an objective convener.

We were fortunate to have such a person in one of our parishioners. Long-range planning had been one of the roles he'd played in a long career as a corporate consultant. He also knew the parish, having been a member for thirty years.

Get everyone on board

I brought the rest of the parish into the process months before we actually met as a committee. I explained the importance, even necessity, of long-range planning in particular.

First, I met with the wardens and explained why I thought now was the time. The three of us then took the idea to the next vestry meeting.

From there we moved out by explaining our proposed plan and process at a vestry/former vestry party. We held these parties every spring at a parishioner's home. They were informal events at which I updated the group on what I felt were currently the key initiatives.

It's good to always keep former members of your vestry on board. It respects their past and current contributions. Plus, they're people who will always be leaders in your church. Other members talk (sometimes complain) to them and look up to them. For the overall good of the church, keep these people in the know.

Expect a lot of questions. A lot of non-corporate types will have only the foggiest, if any, understanding of what long-range planning is.

Whatever you do, don't be in a hurry. Some church leaders make the mistake of trying to introduce something new with a pre-conceived time schedule built in. More important than timing is having your people on board.

Go slow. Explain carefully. Which I next did through a Sunday morning sermon, followed by a Q and A session at the coffee hour after the main service. Then I wrote a letter explaining the process in the parish newsletter. Remember what I learned as a college communications major: *Tell them what you're going to tell them. Tell them. Tell them what you told them.*

Ask people to pray. Enlist the prayer support of individual church members and any prayer and/or small groups you have to pray that God's will be discerned and ultimately accomplished in this new long-range planning process.

Convene the committee and set the guidelines

You'll need to determine the frequency of meetings. At your first meeting, introduce the facilitator as chair. Let him then explain the format you'll be following. Your first meeting will also give you a chance to explain your hopes as rector to the group and give everyone present a chance to express theirs. This is the time for creative license, time to have some fun with the process, to let your and the group's creativity run rampant. Some humor can lighten the feeling of responsibility, open you up to fresh thinking, draw you closer together.

The facilitator and I also introduced to the group our understanding of Appreciative Inquiry and our plan to use it as one of our tools for the process we'd be following.

What exactly is Appreciative Inquiry? This approach was developed at Case Western Reserve University's department of organizational behavior, starting with a 1987 article by David Cooperrider and Suresh Strivastva. They felt that the overuse of "problem solving" hampered any kind of social improvement, and what was needed were new methods of inquiry that would help generate new ideas and models for how to organize.

Appreciative Inquiry is a positive-change management approach that focuses on identifying what is working well, why it's working well ,and then doing more of it. The basic tenet is that an organization will grow in whichever direction people in the organization focus their attention—i.e., as a church, we need to keep our eyes on Jesus, learning his overall vision for every church and his particular vision for St. Matthew's.

Positive questions lead to positive change.

Appreciative Inquiry suggests these four steps to positive change. That's what I was committed to seeing happen now in our long-range planning process:

- First, *discover*. Appreciate and value the best of what exists now. Gather information and stories around what is working well now.

- Second, *dream*. Envision what might be.

- Third, *design*. Determine what could be.

- Fourth, *deliver*. Innovating what will be.

As we explained this overall approach to our newly formed committee, I could sense their shared relief. The idea of looking for the positive seemed to reduce the anxiety some members had that we might turn over stones that concealed negative feelings held by some of their fellow parishioners.

Starting from Day One with the stated intention of looking for, building on, and hoping to achieve all things positive visibly lightened the mood of our meetings. It also raised the bar for us going forward, as in: "Let's see what great things we can make happen for St. Matthew's and the Lord."

With that in mind, we got busy on the all-important next step: The Questionnaire.

Design, distribute, and analyze an all-parish questionnaire

Parishioner input is the most important part of long-range planning. The questionnaire needs to be specific in polling the people on what they like most about their church and finding out what they'd like to see changed, added, or deleted from the existing program.

Again, make sure you've adequately explained that everyone will get a questionnaire, the importance of their filling it out, and the time schedule.

We were fortunate in getting a very high percentage of responders and a very high positive rating. We also received a few answers that surprised us. One surprise was that more people than I'd expected felt that although we'd made progress our coffee hours were still not as welcoming to newcomers as they should be. Another surprise was the large number of people who advocated for our starting a pre-school, which had been a non-disclosed dream of mine since my first visit to the church. We also had a lot of requests for the addition of an afternoon Sunday Communion service.

When months later we finally completed a successful planning process, these were the primary changes we were able to put into place. We encouraged, and monitored, more welcoming involvement in the coffee hours. We started a five o'clock Sunday service. And two years later, after much planning and research, we opened the St. Matthew's School for two-, three-, and four-year-olds.

These have all proven successful. But in some ways, the most positive of all was that the parishioners felt uniquely heard, therefore in some ways valued as never before.

NOTE: Another surprise, and an embarrassing one for me as rector, came when in our committee I brought up what I felt was the key issue of personal discipleship, and most of the committee had no idea what discipleship is. I was mortified. How had I managed to be these people's spiritual leader all these years and somehow not taught them the meaning of discipleship? Reminder for me, for all of us: *take nothing for granted.*

To summarize, the five steps of a successful long-range plan are:

- Explain the importance of long-range-planning.
- Listen to your parishioners.
- Process the information they give you.

- Formulate a plan.
- Execute the plan.

Yours will be a healthier church for all this time and loving care you've given it.

QUESTION 23

DO I HAVE TO ATTEND ALL LAY LEADERSHIP MEETINGS AND ALL PARISH EVENTS?

YES, TO LEADERSHIP MEETINGS

Absolutely. According to the Episcopal Church canons the rector either chairs vestry meetings or delegates it to the senior warden. I always chaired the meetings. Which I recommend unless you're really uncomfortable with it. If you're not Episcopal, you may well have other traditions.

Wardens come and go. For the length of your tenure, *you* are the spiritual leader of the church. Which means you should also to some degree oversee all aspects of parish life, though you'll delegate much of the planning and execution. You can't be involved in everything. But you need to be aware of everything that's happening, from budget planning to maintenance needs, and offer your input as needed.

YES, TO PARISH EVENTS

As chief community builder, you need to be a prime motivator in encouraging and supporting every event.

You'll sign on to the initial idea, support the planning, and encourage the laity and/or assisting clergy who design and implement the events.

Then you'll announce them at Sunday services, make sure they're in the parish mailings—hard copy and online—with a lot of advance warning, and see that the parish understands how important it is for them to attend. One of the worst mistakes is when the promotion doesn't match the planning.

Getting the people there is key. If you don't do that, your event organizers feel deflated and less keen to volunteer for future activities.

It's the rare event that doesn't need and benefit from the senior minister's presence.

TIP: Stay to the end. I always stayed to help with clean-up. You may say, "I'm tired. I've had a long day, been going since early this morning."
So have your lay volunteers.

Unless something unforeseen over which you have no control comes up, plan your day so you can stay with them till the end. I've washed dishes, knocked down folding tables and chairs, and swept the floor. This way, your volunteers feel supported, valued, and feel you're one of them. Which you are.

QUESTION 24

HOW CAN I STAY FRESH THROUGHOUT MY YEARS IN MINISTRY?

BY STAYING CLOSE TO THE LORD

I begin every day with the words, "This is the day the LORD has made. I will rejoice and be glad in it." It gets me going in the right frame of mind. Sometimes I have to say it more than once. On really dark days, I've repeated it as many as five times!

But just saying the words helps remind me that "The joy of the LORD is my strength"; that "The steadfast love of the LORD never ceases. His mercies never come to an end; they are new every morning. Great is thy faithfulness" (Lamentations 3:22–23).

I look to the Bible for reminders of his faithfulness. When I was going through a particularly rough time not long ago, I went to Psalm 18. Here's David thanking God for delivering him at last from Saul. I applied God's saving grace for David to my situation. I read certain passages over and over for weeks until they became mine.

"You rescued me from the fury of my enemies; you exalted me above those who rose against me; you saved me from the deadly foe. Therefore I extol you among the nations, O LORD, and sing praises to your name" (Psalm 18:4–49).

I pray. How often have I prayed in times of stress, fatigue, or dejection, "Lord, renew me, revive me, restore me." There are a lot of great "re-" prefix words.

How often have I prayed when people were being difficult, "Lord, they're yours. *You* deal with them."

How often have I prayed when facing a potentially difficult meeting or an unusually painful pastoral situation, "Lord, please give me the words. Handle this situation through me. Give these people what they need through me. Love them through me. Give me your wisdom and guidance and understanding."

Never once in all these years has he failed me. Always, he's given me what I've needed in the moment.

I didn't decide to be ordained. I answered his call. As long as I remain faithful to the call, and put my trust in him, he will give me what I need to perform the tasks that come my way.

This understanding applies to his giving me the spiritual nourishment and refreshment I need to stay in shape to carry out the tasks he gives me to fulfill.

KEEP LEARNING

I find that ongoing study helps keep me energized. And I've always wanted to keep getting better at what I do.

One of the ways I've continued learning is by studying leaders in other disciplines. Athletic coaches, particularly of team sports, for example, can teach us spiritual leaders a lot. They, like us, are helping form groups of people to work together in achieving agreed-upon, positive goals. Their goal may be winning games. Our goal is making the difference the Lord wants us to make in the community and world he's placed us in.

With that in mind, I particularly valued an article I read in *Sports Illustrated* some time ago. It was an interview with a veteran coach, Indiana University's basketball coach Tom Cream, who, at the age of fifty, lost his job. He made the most of it by taking his own Gap Year. He traveled around meeting with other coaches and observing them interacting with their players.

Tom Cream has the kind of attitude I recommend. He says, "I want to become a better leader, a better manager, a better coach, a better man—by watching the best."

At the end of his study year, Coach Cream summarized some of what he'd learned. It can apply to us as leaders of churches. He says,

> I started this year with no goal other than to learn as much from as many people as I could, to go behind the scenes to see how organizations operate and leaders lead. At times it's been humbling.

I've seen strong management and thought about situations I could have handled better. It's also been validating—Hey, we did that, too or That's how I handled a similar challenge.

But when you have a growth mind-set, you want to incorporate new ideas—and not be afraid to delete old ideas that may no longer be effective.

Tom Cream adds: "And I was reminded that long hours can co-exist with joy."

Yes! How important it is for us to look for the joy ever-present, like an underground stream—especially in the most frustrating, exhausting, and draining situations.

My Tom Cream agenda has included attending informational conferences in churches as different as Willow Creek, outside Chicago, and St. Bartholomew's and Trinity Wall Street Episcopal Churches in New York City. I attended a workshop on Appreciative Inquiry, led by Anglican clergyman and parish consultant Rob Voyle. Two stints at The Oxford Round Table and a month-long clergy course at St. George's House in Windsor Castle proved to be both immensely informational and refreshing.

I don't know about you, but I always find getting away from my usual environment frees me up to new ideas and fresh ways of seeing things. Some of my best ideas have come on airplanes.

STAY IN GOOD PHYSICAL SHAPE

Physical exercise has always been key to my keeping up my energy level. Walk. Go to the gym. Swim. Do whatever works for you. And eat right. Keep your weight under control. You'll be a better witness for the Lord if you do. You'll also maintain a higher level of energy and enthusiasm, and have the reserves you need when you're under stress

So pray. Ask the Lord to show you what he wants you to see in his word. Find ways to get breaks when you can. Do continuing education that interests and energizes you. Stay healthy. Most of all, *depend on him.* Don't try to do it on your own. Remember—he designed us to need him.

So on those days when you're feeling overwhelmed and it all feels like simply too much, give it all to him: "Here, Lord, you take it. Too much for me. If this is going to get done, *you* are going to have to do it."

And he will. Because he's faithful.

QUESTION 25

WHAT ARE THE CHARACTERISTICS OF A HEALTHY CHURCH?

A HEALTHY CHURCH IS A COMMUNITY OF BELIEVERS WHO UNDERSTAND THAT ITS NUMBER-ONE PURPOSE IS CORPORATE WORSHIP

In the words of The Westminster Confession: "Man's chief end is to worship God and enjoy Him forever."

Do you enjoy God? Do you enjoy being with him—singly and corporately? In a healthy church, worship is enjoyable. Joyous. Uplifting. Life-enhancing. It's also community-building. Powerful, Spirit-inspired worship deepens our bonds of fellowship.

Praise and worship are designed for us to come before God in thanksgiving, love, and adoration.

There's another purpose. "God *inhabits* the praises of his people." Praise and worship bring God on the scene. We experience his manifest presence. Jesus tells us that whenever two or more are gathered in his name, there he will be in the midst of us. Sometimes corporate worship is so powerful you feel the presence of the Lord in a manifest way. Then the air seems to sparkle like liquid gold. You somehow know he's right there with you. Those are the special times, the remarkable times of worship.

Then the words of the old chorus come to life: "Surely the presence of the Lord is in this place. You can hear the rush of angel's wings; see glory on each face."

A healthy church knows—and lives into with great care and attention to planning and execution—the crucial importance, the primacy, the centrality of worship.

During all the years I was at St. Matthew's, we had as our organist and director of music Anthony Newman, one of the great musicians of our age. Tony is considered one of the all-time great interpreters of Baroque music. He has played concerts around the world. He's made several hundred CDs, his most successful with Wynton Marsalis. Wynton calls Tony "The high priest of Bach."

Tony is also a composer; with a remarkable and ongoing outlay of spectacular music.

One of his unique contributions to our St. Matthew's worship has been his habit of playing the hymns a little faster than you normally hear them played. This helps keeps the energy up. Spare me lugubrious hymns.

Another worship tip: you, not your organist, should choose the hymns. Most organists I've known, by virtue of their talent and training, often prefer hymns that though musically interesting to a lot of parishioners, aren't all that singable. And as much as you can, sing hymns your people know. Then they'll sing out, which keeps the energy up. Poll the congregation when you arrive to discover their favorite hymns. To learn the ones they really enjoy, have the occasional hymn sing at a main service.

Congregational singing is key to inspirational worship. People feel good, they feel happy, when they can boom out the hymns. They feel lost and annoyed when you spring a hymn they've never heard.

Of course, you can't sing from only the same in-house "hymn book" all the time. Some hymns are worth introducing. When you do, announce that here's a new hymn and why it's worth learning. If necessary, get a member or two of the choir up in front to sing it through a couple of times first, so the congregation know how it goes. And avoid the no-melody hymns. They may be musically important, but if your people can't sing them, let the organist play them during communion or some other time the congregation doesn't need to sing.

A HEALTHY CHURCH PUTS A PRIORITY ON LEARNING ABOUT GOD, HIS PLAN AND PURPOSE FOR HIS CHURCH, FOR INDIVIDUAL BELIEVERS, AND FOR THE WORLD

We do that by emphasizing preaching and teaching—especially Bible study. As clergy, we must offer, and stress, the importance of daily Bible reading and weekly corporate study.

As one of my lay mentors for ministry once said, "Terry, your safest, healthiest place to live is in the Bible. You need to move in and take up residence there."

A HEALTHY CHURCH STRESSES THE IMPORTANCE OF OUR ONENESS IN DIVERSITY

This is where we make a powerful counter-statement to today's tragic reversion to white supremacy, anti-Semitism, and racism of all kinds.

In some ways, other than the redeeming love of Christ, that's the most important witness the local church has to make in today's America: our unity in diversity.

We need to keep returning to Paul's declaration in Galatians 3:26–29: "For you are all the children of God by faith in Christ Jesus. For as many of you as have been baptized into Christ have put on Christ. There is neither Jew nor Greek. There is neither bond nor free. There is neither male nor female. For you are all one in Christ Jesus" (King James).

When the first followers of Jesus looked around at each other they were astonished by the diversity among them.

Under the old covenant, God's chosen people had been the Jews. Under the new, of which these original Christians joyously found themselves, there was Greek and Jew, circumcised and uncircumcised, barbarian, Scythian, slave and free (Colossians 3:11). These new chosen of the Lord were amazed. Each of these categories had made for radical segregation in former times.

Now, wonder of wonders, *unity*—not segregation—had become central to the new community. Race, skin color, gender and wealth had formerly placed people on the social ladder. Now, however, unity in Christ had become the basis for accepting each other as equals. As Paul declared, "We, who are many are *one body*" (1 Corinthians 10:17 NIV).

The ordination of women and homosexuals has more lately recognized what God intended from the creation of his body the church. Which is that all ministry is efficacious not because of the gender or sexual orientation of the minister, lay or clergy, but by whether or not the Spirit of God is present within and working through that person. The ultimate question remains, of course, for *all* of us ordained: "Is this the Lord's call?"

Which also means there is no room for sacerdotalism, the uplifting of clergy over lay ministers. Each is equally important.

Each spiritual gift is of equal importance. Some get a lot more show and attention by the nature of their gift. But that does not make them more important in God's eyes or in the working out of his plan through his church. The church depends on every member and the gifts the Lord has given each one of us.

Too much of the world, especially it seems at the time of writing, despises and rejects diversity. It sees those who are racially, ethnically, socially, and sexually different as abhorrent. The ultimate manifestation are the hate-inspired shootings of innocent Americans by hate-filled other Americans.

The Lord, however, delights in the diversity of his creation. That's why his created order, human and inanimate, is infinitely, gloriously, endlessly diverse.

The church was not intended to be some kind of club made up of similar people but rather a richly varied yeasty mix, a cross section of all humanity.

As church leaders we need to help our people understand, celebrate, practice, and proclaim to the world around us the wonders of diversity. It is one of the greatest gifts we have to offer this current age.

A HEALTHY CHURCH IS A COMPASSIONATE CHURCH

Jesus is our model for caring for others both within and without our community. During his earthly ministry he taught by teaching and example the necessity of reaching beyond our own needs and those of family and friends to help others in distress.

He told his followers they must feed the hungry, give drink to the thirsty, shelter the homeless, clothe the naked, care for the sick, and visit those in prison.

In the Book of Acts we see the first church's masterful creation of a welfare system to help indigent members. The wealthier members of the group turned over cash they didn't need to elders of the group to dispense as needed. Thus no early Christian did without.

No wonder the surrounding pagan communities looked with wonder at these followers of the Nazarene. "Look," they were reported to have said, "how these people love each other!"

May it be said of us in our churches today.

In-church ministry to the hurting of our own community and mission to the greater community beyond our doors are not options. When you study the teaching of Jesus, you see that they are his *orders*, not suggestions to us. "Love others as I have loved you." By which he meant not in word only but also in *action*. Love in action.

And in this ministry of compassion, we realize the joy that returns to us over and above anything we could have thought or imagined.

A HEALTHY CHURCH HELPS TRANSFORM THE CULTURE

Some understanding of church sees the world as an enemy that must be despised, feared, and rejected. That mindset forgets that God so loved the world he sent his Son to die for it (John 3:16).

Another view is the church *of* the world, which sees the church as a part of society—here to play its role, along with other religions, secular organizations, and political movements to help make the world a better place.

There's nothing wrong with that—unless, that is, we lose sight of our distinctive place in the great, overarching, eternal plan of God for his church. Which is that we are called not to become part of the world but to *transform* the world, in his name and by his Spirit.

We must not forget that with all our mission and outreach and positive contributions to the world around us, we are making these positive efforts *in Jesus' name*. We're here always to show him as head of his church wherein peace, justice, equality, and the love and acceptance of others are lived out.

And there's this: as a healthy church we teach and acknowledge and rejoice in the fact that Christ's body, the church, of which we are a part as adopted sons and daughters of God, was planned by him before the foundations of the world and will survive throughout eternity.

HOW CAN A CHURCH
BECOME UNHEALTHY?

WHEN THE SPIRITUAL LEADER IS NOT SUITED TO THE TASK

What do I mean by "unsuited"? Here's an example. One small but vital and beginning-to-grow neighborhood church in suburban Boston called a highly educated, seemingly well-qualified young men as rector. Though he'd never been a rector before, the depth of his training as a clergy assistant and his obvious intelligence and attractive personality seemed to make him an admirable choice.

He started in September. His installation as rector was scheduled for the following January. During that time, all went well. The people were getting to know their new leader. He made no major gaffes. He was a good preacher. The search committee felt confident they'd made a good choice.

Then a few days before the installation, a member of the vestry was online and somehow came across the information that their new rector had recently put his name into the running for another, much grander position, half way across the country. He'd been rector for less than six months!

The bishop came and installed the new rector. The parish went through the motions of celebrating his new ministry. Then the vestryman who'd seen the online notice brought it to the vestry.

The vestry reacted with predictable shock, dismay, and sorrow. The bishop was brought in. The new rector was ultimately removed from his position by the bishop.

And the church sank into months of gloom and depression. The spark had gone out of their common life. The vestry had no energy for another search so soon. The bishop appointed a young man as interim rector to serve for as long as it took for the church to work through its feelings of hurt and betrayal.

If the church had been older and more firmly settled in its internal identity and sense of self as a community, it likely would have been better able to handle the rejection. As it was, several members left to join other churches and it has taken years for the church to find its way back to the healthy condition it had previously enjoyed.

Another situation was one in which an extremely self-centered rector was chosen. He, like the young rector who was forced to resign, saw his new call as a steppingstone to greater things. He was also limited in his areas of giftedness. He had only one of the several gifts it takes to be a successful rector. Leadership was not among them. Neither was pastoral care. He would probably have made a better supporting player on a multi-clergy staff.

As it was, his self-centeredness played itself out over time in an inability to relate to the parishioners. They felt he had no interest in them, that he was there to be the center of attention.

The difference was that in this case the bishop didn't remove the rector. Stewardship fell markedly. Many people left the church. Once healthy, it adapted a kind of bunker mentality, as in "we'll just have to wait this out." Meanwhile, much of the life and energy of the community were dissipated. The man finally left, but it has taken a long time for the church to return to its former health and vitality.

A third example is a small-town church, with a history that dates to before the Revolutionary War.

In this case, the sickness did not originate with the clergy leader but with a handful of lay leaders bent on destruction.

In two back-to-back cases, this small group turned first on one rector, then on her successor, and by an unconscionably cruel and vindictive smear campaign drove each in succession out of the church.

Evil prevailed. I don't know if the church has recovered or not.

Another energy-zapper can be clergy leadership that, if not narcissistic, may be engaged in some kind of dysfunctional or unacceptable practice that some, if not all, parishioners are aware of but keep silent about.

One word that can be used to describe an unhealthy church is lackluster. The energy, sense of unity in purpose, and joy are missing. What's left is a tragic, lifeless form of church—a non-sequitur, as by definition the church is Christ's living, breathing, Spirit-filled body—infused by his life and bringing his life, his hope, and his love to the world.

PART 3

MANAGEMENT

QUESTION 27

HOW DO I EFFECTIVELY MANAGE STAFF?

IT HELPS TO HAVE THE RIGHT PEOPLE IN THE RIGHT POSITIONS

In the words of Jim Collins in his classic *Good to Great*, "get the right people on the bus." As in the corporate world, so our non-profit needs are basically the same. You try to find the people with the appropriate skills who, hopefully, will fit your needs and the culture of the church.

It's nice when it works. Of course, you think you've always hired the right person for the job. Time will tell if you have.

BOTH LEAD AND MANAGE

I was fortunate in one of my pre-ministry careers to be the managing editor of a national magazine. A lot of what I did in that job prepared me to manage a parish (not to be confused with leading a parish; management being one aspect of leadership).

As managing editor, my responsibilities were overseeing the staff (including hiring and when necessary firing), budgets, and monitoring the process of every issue of the magazine from initial planning stages through the steps of writing and editing and laying out the articles until we held the printed product in our hand. That meant I had to see that the writers, artists, and layout designers, proof readers, and people who printed the magazine worked together smoothly.

One of the things I learned was that every person on the staff had the talent and responsibility for their one aspect of the issue. Not surprisingly, they also tended to think their part was the most important: whether writing, editing, design, proof-reading, or printing.

Which meant they were less inclined to look at the overall product. That's up to the editor—who sits above it all and envisions every new issue and the long-range purpose and impact of the magazine. It's also up to the managing editor, my job, who serves the editor in making sure his or her vision is carried out to maximum impact.

As rector, you're both editor and managing editor: responsible for both the parish vision and for its fulfillment.

Increasingly, through the years as rector, I depended on my superb parish administrator to handle the day-by-day job of managing the lay staff, though it was clear that, ultimately, she and all the other staff members reported to me.

CONVEY THE VISION TO YOUR STAFF AS WELL AS TO THE ENTIRE PARISH

Your responsibility is The Three C's of Visioning, something I learned from Bill Hybels, then senior pastor of Willow Creek Church. They are: catch, cast, and carry. *Catch* the vision from God. *Cast* the vision in a sufficiently winsome way for the people to buy into it. *Carry out* the vision.

As leader, you obviously can't carry out the vision on your own. It's your role to enlist the parishioners, who will make it happen.

These are always the leader's responsibility. Though they have dramatically different parts to play, for the goals to be successfully realized, both your staff and the majority of parishioners need to enthusiastically buy into the vision.

Since the lay staff don't sit in on vestry meetings and usually don't attend church services, you have to do the same kind of work with them you do with the parish at large. You have to help them see why the church exists in the first place, where it's going, and help them understand their role in achieving the Lord's goals.

One thing I've always told my colleagues is that though they may disagree with, even argue with, a decision I make, I always have a *reason* for making it. Not for me the approach that says, "We'll do it because I said we'll do it." No.

"It" may originate in my gut, or as some fleeing, half-formed idea. In either case, it is hopefully God-inspired. But by the time I put it into practice I've done the preparation—whatever it may take—to be able to explain the rationale.

That applies to your vestry or board and to the church at large. I've seen rectors short-change their effectiveness with entire congregations by not adequately explaining the rationale for an unpopular decision they've foisted on the people. The people may not agree with something you're doing, but they'll thank you for doing your best to explain why you're doing it. Effective communication builds trust.

When it comes to lay staff, such rationalizing on your part will be harder for some to comprehend than for others. For one reason, because some will be more churched than others. I've always hired Christians for lay staff positions, because they're already part of the body of Christ—whatever their denomination or lack of—and are therefore pre-disposed to understanding why we're here doing what we're doing.

That does not mean, however, that you should automatically bar a non-Christian from filling some appropriate position.

TEACH WHAT IT MEANS TO WORK FOR A CHURCH

I found my chief opportunity for goal-setting, follow-up, and feedback were our weekly staff meetings. I impressed on them the importance of their contributions, reminded them that we all were here to serve the Lord and his people, and were involved in furthering the greatest cause there is.

Practically, I helped them see that when it comes to parishioners, we're like an in-house P.R. agency: serving the clients (parishioners) and doing our best to support them and their ministries as laity.

I told my staff they should never argue with a parishioner; if someone gets pushy, difficult, or mean-spirited, I said they should come to me for intervention. In all my years of managing staff, that never happened.

I also impressed on them the need for excellence. I learned that from the first rector I served under. Excellence comes in many forms. From precision in liturgy to not launching so many parish activities that some suffer from lack of planning to pastoral care.

Excellence needs to extend to the physical plant. Unpainted, shabbily maintained buildings and grounds send the message that the people in this church don't value the Lord very highly. I make allowance for churches who are strapped financially, though parishioners are usually happy to help paint, repair, and clean up. For example, before I became rector, our church initiated Project SMILE, a lay group that saved money by taking over certain painting projects and repairs.

We need to do whatever it takes to keep our plant looking as good as possible.

I carried that down to very small details. Maybe it reflects my obsessive nature. But I always impressed on my staffs that we are here as representatives of Jesus to welcome all who enter in his name. We need to offer the spiritual gift of hospitality. Which means all of us who work in the facilities need to develop the habit of neatness—not just in our individual offices but in the rest of the parish house.

How many times have I hauled off dead bouquets from the front desk, picked up paper towels from the men's room floor, carted off midnight-run boxes dropped at the door to the closet we stored them in.

In an active church, as staff—lay and clergy—you need to be willing to mind the details every day, all the time. You're welcoming every visitor, church member, and others, on the Lord's behalf.

BUILD POSITIVE STAFF RELATIONSHIPS

When I was associate rector of Christ Church in Greenwich, we had a big staff—twenty-three, including lay and clergy. The rector appreciated the importance of collegiality. Along with weekly staff meetings, we had staff birthday lunches and quiet days of prayer and reflection in Advent and Lent. When some staff conflicts threatened to get out of hand, he initiated what we jokingly referred to as "Rocky Road," group therapy with a local psychologist! That rector appreciated what he called "healthy friction" more than I do. He sometimes criticized me for avoiding conflict. But sometimes conflict won't avoid you, so be prepared to handle it when necessary.

Mostly, my experiences of managing and leading staff have been smooth and rewarding. With some notable exceptions. One was when I had to plan and carry out an intervention. It was hard work for me and painful for the staff member. But the intervention proved successful. Another was when a staff member needed an intervention, refused the help, and I had to let the person go. I've also had to do occasional bouts of conflict resolution, but very few considering the numbers of years and number of staff I've managed.

CHERISH YOUR STAFF

Show them you value not only their contributions, you value *them*. Learn about their families and ask them about their lives outside their job. Show them you find them interesting as people, not only as co-workers.

I've seen leaders pour on the charm to their parishioners and toughen up with their staffs. Your staff deserve as much respect as your parishioners. A rough management style is not only unChristian, it's also not smart. You need to know they have your back, and they need to know you have theirs. We need to be in each other's corner. It's about mutual trust. Nobody who doesn't feel safe can do their best job.

BE VULNERABLE

Along with trust comes your need to occasionally show your own vulnerability. By that I don't mean whining to your staff. I don't mean using them as your shrink. I certainly don't mean forming any kind of inappropriately intimate relationships. What I mean is that you may from time to time need to admit, "I blew that one!" Or "I'm not sure." Don't be afraid to take responsibility for making a mistake. It's okay to say, "I don't know," okay to ask them for help.

By letting yourself be vulnerable it frees them to accept their own vulnerability. And we're all vulnerable. I was raised in an era that to show vulnerability was weakness. I was supposed to have all the answers—or at least act like I did.

That attitude on a leader's part can be reassuring to some. But it can also be intimidating or off-putting to others.

When you occasionally show your vulnerability, it helps your staff feel safe, understood, accepted by you. If they see you accepting your imperfections, they're better able to accept theirs and feel freer to do their best.

As Bene Brown says in her landmark *Dare to Lead*, "There is no daring leadership without vulnerability." (New York: Random House, 2018, p. 35.)

She describes the phenomenon of "'armoring,' the self-protective thoughts, emotions and behaviors we develop to protect ourselves from our own vulnerability. . . . When our organization rewards armoring behaviors like blaming, shaming, cynicism, perfectionism, and emotional stoicism we can't expect innovative work. You can't fully grow and contribute behind armor. It takes a massive amount of energy just to carry it around—sometimes it takes all our energy." (ibid. p. 14.)

Google says its most productive teams enjoy a feeling of what they term "psychological safety," which results from workers feeling their input is welcomed and valued. Research from a broad variety of sources confirms Google's findings.

Sam Walker, writing in *The Wall Street Journal*, says, "Happy workers not only score higher for engagement, productivity, loyalty, creativity, they take fewer sick days and are more likely to help their colleagues." ("Gratitude Is Good for Business," *The Wall Street Journal*, November 24–25, 2018, p. B1.)

Your staff is the community within the community. Though you're not their pastor, there will be times when they'll need you to help them through painful situations: either on the job or personally.

HAVE FUN

As I always told my staffs: "We're all here to serve the Lord and make this the church he wants it to be. That takes all of us, and all of us working together. We're all going to do our best, and we're going to have fun doing it."

Working in a church, despite the frustrations and sometime tragedies should be primarily a joyful experience.

FIVE MANAGEMENT POINTS TO REMEMBER

Help staff identify and develop their gifts.

Empower them by asking them to share their input and opinions. Be willing to listen. Steve Jobs said, "It doesn't make sense to hire smart people and then tell them what to do; we hire smart people, so they can tell us what to do." (*The Week Magazine*, August 20, 2018.)

Expect—and reward—excellence.

Show and tell them how important they are, to you and to the church. Help them appreciate that you have a shared purpose.

Affirm a job well done. Don't forget to thank them for their contributions. Research shows that specific thanks means more to people than does general thanks. In other words, "Great job!" is good. "Great job of getting the budget in on time!" is even better.

Some of my staff have become friends for life.

QUESTION 28

HOW DO I MANAGE CLERGY ASSISTANTS?

Some, but not all, the guidelines for working with lay staff apply to your assisting clergy. Here are some that don't.

LOOK FOR BALANCE

Balance in age and gender. I always had two assisting clergy. One was a young man just out of seminary. The other a woman, all but one with teen-aged children. I was the oldest.

Hire to balance your weaknesses. Nobody has all the gifts. When looking for a clergy assistant, try to find someone who has at least some of the traits you don't.

For example, I've always said I don't like to think. I'd rather act than think. An exaggeration, of course, yet I'm a man of ideas and action more than of contemplation.

I've been fortunate to find clergy assistants who were both more intellectual and contemplative than I. Their sermons, teaching, and approach to counseling reflected these gifts and were appreciated by parishioners who valued these traits.

HIRE COLLEAGUES MORE FOR THEIR GIFTS THAN TO FILL A MINISTRY SLOT

Encourage the development of those gifts.

One of the greatest leadership talents of my mentor Jack Bishop was to identify and help release the gifts of his fellow clergy.

I likened him to a man walking down a city street. It's a cold day and you see puffs of steam rising from holes in manhole covers. Jack comes along and screws off the covers to let the full steam rise like a mini geyser.

He encouraged us and gave us the freedom to try new things, explore fresh ideas. Some didn't pan out. Some did. And when they did, we his associates, Jack, and the church benefited.

Certain ministries have to be covered, of course: youth, outreach, adult education, fellowship, and fund-raising events. The bigger the church, the more the senior pastor has to assign his or her clergy to oversee certain activities.

But it's good, when possible, to discuss the unique interests your assistant or assistants may have, so they can work with ministries that match their interests and abilities.

Motivate and encourage them to develop their passions. For example, I gave my first female clergy assistant free reign to launch a new-mothers' ministry. She had a toddler. She started a weekly get-together for mothers of small children.

A few years later, I hired another female assistant who had a passion for children. I assigned what became for her the weekly joy of leading the worship service for our pre-school children, ages two to four. Her creativity blossomed!

A gift for teaching? Find ways to make it happen. Men's ministry? Let's try something that's never been tried.

Love liturgy? Yes, the planning and execution of liturgies are the rector's responsibility. But when we started a five o'clock Sunday service, I delegated it to first one, then when he left, another of my young male assistants.

They ran their ideas by me, of course, and I led the service once every six weeks. But I encouraged them to explore options, try things that had never been done before in our very liturgically traditional church. They did, and the people who attended loved it.

I also encouraged the former to introduce two new Holy Week services, which also proved successful.

His successor took the five o'clock service to new heights of creativity. He introduced a regularly scheduled Celtic worship service. And even a Halloween service from our *Episcopal Book of Occasional Services*—which I hadn't known existed. He also came up with a variety of music ideas—from the traditional organ to a guitarist who led contemporary songs, a cellist, and one time a Black Gospel choir.

Freedom within limits. Push out the boundaries. You can try anything once. And, as I told them, "Some will work and some won't, but you've had the fun, and learning, of trying."

HIRE PEOPLE YOU WANT TO SPEND TIME WITH

When I answered the call to assist John Harper on Lafayette Square, he said, "Terry, I'm not just hiring you to serve here. I'm hiring you to be a friend." We did form a friendship that lasted until his death many years later.

When you enjoy positive relationships with your clergy colleagues, everyone benefits. You, the clergy, and also the parishioners. They pick up the warmth and affection you have for each other. You model Christian love and mutual respect, which helps your people feel safe.

VALUE THEIR OPINIONS.

Ask them what they think about what's happening in the church, with certain issues and parishioners.

Always treat them as colleagues, never subordinates, though times may arise when you have to exert your authority and seniority. This almost never happened with me. When it does, explain your rationale. They are, after all, there to learn from you. Mentoring is a crucial aspect of the senior pastor's role.

Despite your greater knowledge and experience, be prepared to learn from them. One of the most fun I had with an assistant was arguing theology with her. One memorable topic: works righteousness vs. grace.

STAY CONNECTED

Meet with your assistants, at least briefly, every day and once a week to discuss pastoral issues and the upcoming Sunday services.

Never hold yourself apart. With your clergy as well as your lay staff, keep an open door, an open mind and an open heart.

WHAT ARE SOME TIPS ON RUNNING A MEETING?

LEARN THE BASICS

When I became rector, I realized that though I'd run meetings for many years in a variety of positions I'd never had training on the so-called correct way.

Before my first vestry meeting as rector, I went to the library and checked out a copy of *Robert's Rules and Orders*. I picked up a few details, which made me feel more secure in the presence of some then-intimidating vestry members. They didn't stay intimidating. My first meeting went fine.

GET THERE EARLY

Some years ago, I read an essay on the importance of arriving early—early for a lunch or dinner; early to catch a plane, most importantly for you as leader, early for a meeting, especially one you're chairing. The author made the excellent point that when you get where you have to be early, you avoid feeling rushed and you are then in, rather than out of, control. You have time to gather your thoughts, to think about the goals and objectives you hope to achieve. You avoid unnecessary stress. Reading that essay was a game-changer for me. My habit had been to get to meetings and other engagements on time. But never early; with no time to spare. I was like the baseball player sliding into home plate at the last second before the catcher had the ball. I got home safe, but barely. What a relief I felt going forward when I'd learned and consistently applied my newly discovered *get-there-early* principle. I highly recommend it.

START ON TIME

From the first, I started out with one rule of my own. I determined from the outset that I would start every meeting on the stroke of the hour set. I've done it for the vestry, staff, and every other meeting I've led through the years. I don't wait. Everyone may not be there. I start anyway.

Why so rigid? As I've always said, our time is precious. Sometimes you may be unavoidably detained. But if you know the leader starts promptly, you'll do what it takes to be there.

I've been on boards that gathered at the set time and then would take ten or more minutes to stand around and chat. I say, come early or stay late if you want to chat. The meeting time is the time to conduct our business.

MANAGE THE TIME

Another thing, and you have to sort of intuit this: don't let people run on too long. Some will love the sound of their own voice, others will chase hairs that can deep six the agenda item you're trying to cover. People need to be heard. But not to excess. How do you know when to cut someone off, albeit politely and lovingly? It will depend on the person and the situation of the moment. Practice, practice, practice.

MIND THE DISRUPTERS

A potential distraction can be members whispering among themselves. My way of handling that is to say, in the kindest way of course, "We need to have one conversation at a time, please."

When I was associate rector, the rector and I became aware of a little negative activity among a few vestry members at the opposite end of the table from where we sat. If they disagreed with a position being voiced, we'd see them shaking their heads and rolling their eyes at each other. Then the rector had an idea: he and I would split up. He sent me to the opposite end next to "the grumblers." No more grumbling. They began voicing, or swallowing, their disagreements. The whole tenor of the meetings became more positive.

Over time, you'll find what works and what doesn't. But this is one time when you as leader are the one who both sets the tone and keeps the meeting on course. One thing is sure, most people will thank you for keeping the meetings on point.

PART 4

PEOPLE

QUESTION 30

HOW DO I DEAL
WITH DISMISSIVE PARISHIONERS?

DON'T TAKE IT PERSONALLY

If you're like me, you may have to overcome your need to be liked by everybody. Because you're not going to be, human nature being what it is. So try not to get hung up on being liked. Focus, instead, on your ministry of service—to the Lord and to his people. And if you don't have it naturally, ask the Lord to help you grow a thick skin.

POSSIBLE REASONS

Parishioners may be dismissive or even unfriendly to their rector because:

- They've been hurt or felt let down by the former rector or by clergy somewhere in their past; feel that for some reason they can't trust any of us.

- They need more personal attention from their rector than you can, or should, give them.

- They're mad at God for some unanswered prayer, loss, or tragedy, and are taking it out on you, the Lord's earthly representative.

- They don't like the way you're doing something. Who knows? This option runs the gamut, from the hymns on Sunday morning, to something you've said in a sermon, to some decision you've made that— unknown to you, if they've never verbalized it—has annoyed them.

- Maybe—sorry to say—there's something about you they just don't like, that rubs them for whatever reason. Maybe it's your accent!

One elderly lady, a regular at our eight o'clock service, treated me with unusual coldness. Every time I'd shake hands with her at the door after the service, she'd greet me with a scowl and perfunctory, "Good morning."

I, on the other hand, always gave her my best smile and said, "Good morning, Bunny," with all the warmth I could muster.

Finally, one morning when she obviously couldn't stand it anymore, she growled: "My name's Bambi."

Quickly, I said, "Oh, here's my wife behind you. Rabbits are her signature animal. Sometimes we call her Bunny. I just looked at her and blipped. I'm so sorry."

No quarter given, the lady crowed triumphantly: "You've called me Bunny ever since the day you met me." And off she stormed.

I called her Bambi ever after. We became great friends. We had lots of fun talks. When a few years later she died, I was holding her hand near the end.

The moral: you may never know for sure why a parishioner is upset or how a relationship might improve. That's why we need to keep our eyes on Jesus and on the mission.

QUESTION 31

I FEEL DRAWN TO CERTAIN INDIVIDUALS AND FAMILIES MORE THAN OTHERS. IS THIS NORMAL?

ABSOLUTELY! IT'S NORMAL TO BE DRAWN MORE TO SOME THAN OTHERS

Personal chemistry being what it is, you can't help it. Your responsibility is handling it in such a way that other members of your church don't feel hurt or slighted.

We need to work scrupulously at making every parishioner feel special and important to us, as they are to the Lord. We need to be careful not to show partiality to any one person or group. This is particularly important, even crucial, if your parish has a wide economic range.

I've always doubled my efforts to treat the non-pledger or the less wealthy parishioners the same way I treat our biggest givers.

I remember once visiting an older couple in their home. After the niceties were covered, she said, "I've felt I never really fit in at our church because we're not as wealthy as other people."

From that moment, I upped my efforts to give them attention and pastoral care. That's happened several times through the years. Sometimes I've seen or heard of rectors lavishing their attention on the wealthiest members of their congregations and short-changing the less affluent. It makes me cringe. We need to work hard to avoid it. Obviously, we have our role model in Jesus.

Having said that, Nancy and I have always had parishioners who also became social friends. Some have become friends for a lifetime. You can't expect to move into a community where you know no one and not make friends. And since you're so busy giving time to your church, the parishioners are the first people you're going to meet and the ones you see most.

An exception is if you have children in a local school. As we know, meeting parents through our children can be a great way to make friends. By the time I became a rector, our children were in college.

I have a caveat about making friends of your parishioners. It's this: when I'm with them in a social situation, I never forget that though I may be their friend I'm also they're rector. That means I can never let myself be quite as free with them in some ways as I am with my family or friends outside the church. It may feel restrictive, but so it needs to be. When I first put on the clergy collar, I put on responsibility to behave and express myself in certain ways. Ways that never reflect poorly on the Lord.

QUESTION 32

I SEEM TO BE EXPERIENCING SOME CONFLICT WITH A PARISHIONER. HOW DO I RESOLVE IT?

FACE IT HEAD-ON

I can recall only four actual conflicts with parishioners.

Each was markedly different. Two proved unresolvable, for reasons having to do with the personalities involved.

Two situations I was able to resolve by calling the people into my office and addressing the issue directly. I invited them in, opened with prayer, briefly stated how I saw the conflict and my take on what had happened. Then I invited them to express their feelings on the matter.

Before the meeting, I searched my soul. We always have to do that. We need to ask the Lord to show us how we might be at fault. Is there some hang-up or personal prejudice of mine that's gotten in the way? Has my ego been injured? Do I feel backed into a corner or threatened by the person or situation?

These freeing, prayerful questions need to take place before the meeting, so you can walk in with as clear a conscience as possible.

DON'T BE AFRAID OF ANGER—YOURS OR THEIRS

But remember to keep your cool, not lose control, and trust the Lord to resolve the problem—or not. I was fortunate in both cases that were resolved. We listened to each other. We had our say. We both felt heard by the other. We agreed to move on. We ended up friends.

Some conflicts will not be resolved so easily, if at all. If you're sure in your heart that by prayer and sincerely addressing the difficulty you've done your best, then you have to be willing to let the other person deal with the situation as they are able. Which may, sadly, sometimes end in their leaving the church.

Only one person left the church in the years I was rector. He made the decision, based on a variety of issues, some of which I never fully understood. After he angrily announced his decision to leave, I wrote him a letter thanking him for his numerous contributions to the church, telling him I'd miss having him and his family with us, and wishing them all well. I didn't ask him to return; his leave-taking was too dramatic, his anger too intense.

DON'T TAKE ABUSE

We give everything we can to our parishioners, while maintaining healthy boundaries and healthy interactions, but we are not called to be abused by them. I will accept situational anger from a parishioner. I will not accept abuse. Neither should you. And you should convey the message to your staff—lay and clergy.

There will be the occasional cranky parishioner who will try to take out their anger or frustrations on you. Don't let them get to you. Listen and move on. Commend them to the Lord and pray they get the help they need and the healing he has for them.

QUESTION 33

I'M FEELING MYSELF BEING DRAWN INTO SEVERAL PASTORAL SITUATIONS THAT ARE WEIGHING HEAVILY ON MY HEART. HOW DO I DEAL WITH THEM?

PRAYERFULLY

People have frequently asked me how I deal with all the sadness, heartache, and sometimes tragedy of parish ministry.

Mostly I've handled the burdens of pastoral care by prayer. I give the beloved and their needs to the Lord. I entrust them and their situation to him. I pray he will give them what they need. Which he alone best knows. I may *think* I know what a parishioner needs in any given pastoral situation. It may seem obvious. But there may well be underlying emotional, psychological, physical, or historical issues at play that I can't possibly know. Sometimes, the parishioner involved won't know what these issues are either—because they're repressed for some reason. Pray the Lord will give them what they need and that he will help them through to a better place.

CARE, BUT DON'T CARRY

If I carried their needs as a burden, I'd have burned out and left the ministry years ago. I could never have taken it. The emotional pain can be too intense, sometimes overwhelming.

Yes, there will be the exceptional times when you are going to feel burdened by the awful things happening to people you love and who have been entrusted into your pastoral care. You can't avoid it. The death of a child is the worst I've encountered—sadly, several times.

There are going to be other situations that draw more than your usual emotional energy.

Give them your best as you are able. Visit the sick, the elderly, the lonely, the isolated. Show them you care. Never be in a hurry, but don't stay too long either. They may be trying to be "up" for you, but we don't want to exhaust them. Always pray for them before you leave.

And pray specifically; I've found people prefer concrete prayers to vague, hyper-spiritual ones. Meet people where they are. Name the problem they need resolved. If they're sick, don't be afraid to mention the illness. If they're struggling in a relationship, pray for that relationship and for the other person. Entrust them to the Lord. Thank him for answering the prayer, that he might be glorified.

QUESTION 34

WHAT ABOUT MY USE OF ALCOHOL IN SOCIAL SETTINGS WITH PARISHIONERS AND AT PARISH FUNCTIONS?

THE OPERATIVE WORD IS, SPARINGLY

At a parish event in which I'm expected to say a few words, I never have a glass of wine before I talk. I need to be in full control of my faculties. I may have one glass after, but never before and never more than one.

When at a parishioner's house, exercise control. We all know what that means.

Again, we need to never forget that wherever we are, in whatever situation we find ourselves, we represent the Lord. That means go easy with the liquor.

QUESTION 35

ONE OF MY STAFF COMES TO ME AND SAYS A PARISHIONER IS EXPRESSING DISSATISFACTION WITH ME. WHAT DO I TELL THEM?

TELL YOUR STAFF MEMBER TO REFER THE PARISHIONER TO YOU

Start by thanking your associate for telling you. In rector/staff relationships, as in every relationship, trust is everything. Hopefully you have staff you can depend on to be loyal to you. It's hard to know when we hire someone. I've had plenty of people in my life who have proven disloyal. But as far as I know, no member of any of my staffs has been.

Once when I was newly called to a church as associate, I discovered a member of the rector's staff was routinely bad-mouthing him to people in the parish. Without telling him that, as I didn't feel it was up to me (or looking back, maybe it was), I did tell him that he could trust me to be loyal to him and promised I'd let him know anything I heard that he might want to deal with directly.

Give me the truth. I'd rather have someone come to me and tell me what they don't like or something they disagree with than sounding off about me to other people behind my back. You can't always ensure this, of course. There will be those who need to sound off and air their grievances to whoever will listen. But you need to encourage openness and transparency at every level.

Staff may think they're protecting you by not telling you. But trying to stem the negative energy tends to strengthen not dissipate it.

QUESTION 36

AS YOU LOOK BACK, ARE THERE PASTORAL SITUATIONS YOU FEEL YOU COULD HAVE HANDLED BETTER?

I COULD HAVE HANDLED A LOT OF THINGS BETTER THAN I DID

Here are the worst I can remember, the conflict situations that proved unsolvable.

The first happened several years before I became a rector. I was still in my early forties. The rector I worked for, knowing I had a special affection for elderly people, assigned me several to visit regularly.

One was Dorothy, quite elderly, who has since died. When I knew Dorothy, she had long been widowed. She had no children or any other family. She was mostly bed-ridden and lived alone except for a care-giver.

Dorothy formed an attachment to me. I would take Communion to her bedside. I would ask her questions about her earlier years growing up in the town I'd recently come to. She was charming, an entertaining raconteur, and she determined we'd have a special relationship. I in turn felt desperately sorry for her lonely situation. NOTE: Look out for the "special" relationships.

Discovering I'd done a lot of singing in my youth, she began asking me to sing a hymn for her before I left. Which after we had a chat and I administered Holy Communion, I did. I found it a little embarrassing, but there was no one to hear me but Dorothy and her care-giver invariably watching television in another room. So I complied.

She began to call me the son she'd never had.

One day I found Dorothy in a state of distress. She explained that her yard man would not be able to come the following weekend, and she felt distraught because it was late October, the leaves were piling up, and her lawn, which she loved observing in all seasons from her bedroom windows, was not in the spiff condition she liked.

I had an idea. I told her I'd get a crew from church to come over that Saturday and do the yardwork. She was overjoyed.

I convened several men from the young couples' group I headed. We descended on Dorothy's yard and had fun making it look as good as we could. I had to leave before the final cleanup was completed. But I shared with other guys Dorothy's stern edict that for the leaves to be picked up by the service provided by the town, they had to be bagged and piled in a certain place. They agreed.

The following Monday morning, Dorothy called. I can honestly say no one has ever spoken to me with such vituperative anger as she did that day. My role as surrogate son and clergy troubadour were gone for good. I had "Swiss cheese for brains." I was a turn-coat, a traitor. I'd deliberately left the bagged leaves in the wrong place. She now had to wait another whole week for them to be picked up. The tirade went on, growing increasingly venomous.

When she paused for breath, I said, "I'm sorry we let you down. The guys were there because we all wanted to help you."

I hung up. That was it for my pastoral relationship with Dorothy. I was hurt, infuriated. I handed her off to a clergy colleague and never went near her again.

And she never contacted me.

Obviously, she was a troubled old lady. It would have been more mature of me to sit down and write a detailed farewell letter—explaining my affection and concern for her, apologizing again for the unintended mix-up with the leaf bags, recommending the colleague I was assigning to visit her. I didn't. I was too hurt and angry.

On the other hand, that's when I developed my oft-repeated axiom that applies to all of us—lay and clergy—who serve in a church. Which is that though we've been called to work with and minister to the parishioners, we're not called to be abused by them.

The other "unsolvable" happened like this. A parishioner, up to now very active, angrily took me to task for a slight he'd received from another parishioner. I didn't see what had taken place. Nor did I have time to respond. He charged at me after church one Sunday announced he and his family were leaving the church. And they did.

I didn't call him either. I did, however, go the other step I wish I'd taken with Dorothy. I wrote a conciliatory letter in which I apologized on behalf of the offending party, though I hadn't been present when the perceived abuse occurred. I thanked him for all that he and his family had contributed to our church through their years of membership. I told him I hoped he'd reconsider and come back. But that was it. I didn't call on him. I didn't beg him to return. Looking back, I feel I should have talked to him and his wife in person, because both had been active members of the church.

QUESTION 37

HOW CAN MY CHURCH
WELCOME NEWCOMERS?

PLANNING

You need a welcome committee or commission whose responsibility it is to do the planning necessary to welcome first-time visitors and help them become happily active members.

I was fortunate to identify and enlist competent and committed parishioners, men and women who felt called to this ministry. We met monthly to strategize.

Our program every year, though tweaked over time, was basically the same.

WARMTH

It all begins, of course, with Sunday morning. Although some people new in town will call the office to find out things like service times and children's ministries, most first-timers simply show up for Sunday church. I like the term "radical hospitality," which indicates we have to go all-out to be warm and welcoming. We trust the Lord has brought these people to our doors, and even if they never come again, it's our responsibility to welcome them on his behalf.

How does it happen? The ushers need to be schooled to look out for visitors, welcome them warmly before the service, and connect them with newcomer committee members after.

You'll have members of the welcome committee assigned to every Sunday. The ushers need to wear name-tags. Then when you welcome newcomers at the announcement time, which ideally you will, you can steer them to the ushers for any questions.

Either in your announcements or printed in the order of service should be the notice that visitors will find newcomer cards in the pew. Encourage them to fill out the card and drop it in the offering plate when it's passed.

It's the tradition in some churches to have first-time visitors stand at announcement time so they can be recognized. That's fine for extroverts; not so great for shy people. There are those who want to find their way in more quietly.

After church, ideally a member of the committee will walk the visitors to coffee hour. There they'll be greeted at the newcomer table set up at the entrance to the fellowship room. One or two members of the committee greet with handouts about the church and get them to fill out visitor cards if they haven't already done it in church. Visitors will also get a name-tag.

One of the most discouraging things I ever heard—though I'm glad she told me—was from a woman who visited and with whom I had a nice chat at coffee hour. I tried to call her at the number she'd given on her newcomer card. To no avail. I never saw or heard from her again. Until, that is, I saw her in town one day and she said she'd joined a church down the street. Why? because I was the only one at our church who had talked to her. I ratcheted up our greeting process after that.

As I often told my congregation, say hello to people you don't know. The fellowship hour is time to catch up with your friends and also to welcome newcomers.

PROMOTE THE WEARING OF NAME-TAGS.

Name-tags are not just for newcomers but also for your parishioners.

One of my mentors was so pro-name-tag I told him his tombstone would say "Wear a Name Tag."

He was right, though. Even if your church is small, name-tags help people call each other by name and gives newcomers an immediate sense of belonging.

Volunteers made permanent name tags for every adult member. Kept just inside the fellowship room, parishioners put them on at the beginning of coffee hour and took them off on the way out.

Once they'd officially joined the church, new members were given semi-permanent cards with their name in blue type. That was so long-time members would know to give them special attention. At the end of the year, they got new cards in the black type that symbolized long-term membership.

Vestry and Welcome Commission members had their designation printed above their names.

A NAME-TAG TIP: When making one for yourself or someone else, write the name in big, bold, black letters. If you have to look hard at a name-tag, especially on a fellow parishioner whose name you feel you should know, you're defeating one of the purposes of name-tags. One of which is the possibility of greeting as a newcomer someone who has a member of the church for thirty years.

To keep the greeting going, two things happened within the first week of a newcomer's first visit. I or one of my clergy colleagues called to welcome them again, ask if they had any questions and if we could pay a call in their home or in some other venue. Second, our parish secretary sent a welcome letter signed by me.

Then there's the baked goods. I once attended a workshop on how to integrate newcomers. One thing the expert told us was that research shows that every visitor who gets some home-baked delight delivered to their home joins the church.

I told my Welcome Commission that and one lady said, "I love to bake banana bread. I'll take a loaf of banana bread."

Said another woman: "Give me the recipe. I'll help you."

So our banana-bread ministry was launched. And to great success. Until, that is, Martha Stewart joined our church.

Every woman on the commission agreed: "No way I'm taking banana bread to Martha Stewart."

I took the bread.

INFORMATION

At St. Matthew's, membership consisted of filling out the membership card and returning it to the parish office. You did not have to be a confirmed Episcopalian or attend a membership course to be a member. Although such a course was available and encouraged.

Several times a year we offered an Introduction to St. Matthew's meeting after the main service. This was led by the head of the Welcome Commission, the senior warden, the head of our church school, and me.

The senior warden sketched in an overview of how the church functioned and encouraged pledging. The Commission chair described the get-acquainted events that happened in the course of each year. I talked about the history of the church and the other points that set it apart—stressing how happy we were to have them with us, how vibrant a Christian community they were joining, encouraged questions and their attendance at all-parish functions, such as the annual picnic in June, the Spaghetti Supper, and Haunted Hike at Halloween, and Mardi Gras at the end of the season of Epiphany.

Twice a year we hosted in parishioner's homes a Beat the Winter Doldrums dinner—in February and two cocktail parties—in the early fall and late spring.

EDUCATION

Every year my fellow clergy and I taught a course on what it means to be an Episcopalian. Included was what it means to be the member of a local parish church—in this case St. Matthew's. The class did triple duty. It was for members—new and long-term—who wanted to be confirmed in the Episcopal Church; for previously confirmed Episcopalians who wanted to brush up on what they'd learned, likely as teenagers, for their confirmation; and for new members.

It would be good if you could make attendance mandatory, but in our over-scheduled community, I couldn't take the risk of losing new members.

Another educational piece was a film we produced for showing at all newcomer functions. I called it "A Year in the Life of St. Matthew's" and it featured me as voice-over of footage showing St. Matthew's in action during the course of a typical liturgical year.

I gave an informal teaching on the meaning of each liturgical season, while photos featured our worship and activities against the backdrop of nature's seasons in our country setting.

STAY CONNECTED

You don't want to lose new members because they don't feel they belonged.

We started a so-called buddy system. A member of the Welcome Commission made a special connection with a new person or family. Told them they'd see them in church. Made sure they walked them to coffee hour until they felt comfortable on their own. Answered their questions. Helped them find some service activity where they could get involved and get to know other parishioners.

The activities that seemed to work best were coffee hours, committees for women, spring and fall cleanup Saturdays, and the usher corps for the men. The buddy connection officially ended at the end of the first year, assuming the new parishioners felt connected.

As one of my clergy colleagues once said, "Sometimes people will visit your church and they know what they want: good preaching, good music, a good children's ministry, to make new friends. Other times people will visit your church and they don't know what they're looking for. But they have a need, a need that's propelling them." Our work and our prayer is to help them find their own way into our community of worship, service, and love; help them find new ways of connecting with the Lord.

QUESTION 38

HOW DO I INSPIRE PARISHIONERS TO GREATER STEWARDSHIP?

I TEACH AND PREACH STEWARDSHIP AS RESPONSIBILITY, OPPORTUNITY, AND RECIPROCAL GIFT

In the Episcopal Church, as I noted above, the responsibility for parish properties and finances lie with the vestry.

Having said that, whatever your denominational tradition, you'll need to take a leadership role.

STEWARDSHIP HOW-TO

Every church has its own fund-raising style and traditions. At St. Matthew's we always had two members of the vestry named to lead the stewardship effort. The duo tended to change every few years, to offer a fresh approach.

What didn't change, however, were these traditions: The stewardship leaders wrote a request letter to the parish that went out in advance of our Stewardship Sunday, which we held every year on the Sunday closest to All Saints. That day, a parishioner was selected to talk briefly at announcement time about what St. Matthew's meant to him or her. Then a vestry member got up and talked about the nuts and bolts and necessity of pledging.

I always preached—as I say above—on stewardship.

We did these things at all the Sunday services.

Also, the current issue of the parish newsletter carried a lead article indicating our pledge drive dates and goals.

STEWARDSHIP IS BOTH RESPONSIBILITY AND OPPORTUNITY

It's our responsibility as Christians, because God calls us as his stewards to care for his creation, for his church, for each other, and also to give back to him for his untold blessings to us. Witness the concept of tithing.

Stewardship is our opportunity, because as we give to our church and to the mission and ministries of our church, we are taking part in the great, ongoing ministry of the body of Christ here at home and in the world outside our doors. He has enlisted our aid in not only building his church but in making his kingdom a reality. That means doing our part in carrying on his ministry, which is, as Jesus articulated—quoting Isaiah—in his inaugural address: "to heal the broken-hearted and set the captive free."

When the kingdom comes, it makes itself known in lives both spiritually and concretely transformed. The hungry are fed. The needs of the sick are tended to. Those who have been bound in all kinds of ways are set free. People who've never been able to help themselves are lifted up and both helped and taught how to make their lives better.

I always told my members how fortunate we were to be a part of such a warm and thriving and caring Christian community. Some people are inspired to give simply because they love the Lord and their church.

But in the final analysis, I tended to work hardest convincing the people we need to give to our church not only for our needs but for the needs of the world. I probably quoted one of my heroes, the Second World War Archbishop of Canterbury, William Temple, too many times. But he was right when he said, "The church is the only organization created to give itself away."

STEWARDSHIP IS A RECIPROCAL GIFT

When I say "reciprocal gift" I'm talking about the giving principle that is for some people a little harder to absorb than responsibility and opportunity—i.e., the pleasure, the delight, and the joy we get simply from the act of giving. As we know, it really does feel good to give—unselfishly, unsparingly—to the people who need our help and to the great cause of Christ.

ASK AND THANK

Along with preaching, teaching, and inspiring, you need to take the lead. I also sent my own personalized stewardship letter to every member of the congregation. The vestry's letter went out before Stewardship Sunday, mine after.

This is crucial: you also need to send thank you notes in as timely a manner as possible. In my early days as rector, I had the occasional disgruntled parishioner chastising me because they hadn't been thanked as soon as they felt they should have been. With time the vestry and I rectified that. Their and my notes got mailed within ten days of the received pledge.

Another must: you need to write a hand-written line at the bottom of the typed notes—both requesting and thanking. We are, after all, a Christian family. In this case, that means *personalize*.

And a few final notes:

CONSIDER EXISTING STEWARDSHIP PRACTICES

Every church has its style of managing stewardship. When you're new, study what they've been doing and its apparent effectiveness. You'll make changes, but make sure you convince them why you're making them—and then hope they work!

PERSONAL WITNESS

It's important for the leadership to take a public stewardship stand. Every year, we told the parish their vestry and I had already pledged before we asked them to do the same.

When it comes to giving, we can't ask our people to do what we're not doing.

RELATIONSHIP-BUILDING

As in every aspect of parish ministry, stewardship is about relationships. The more involved people are in their church, the more motivated they are to give. Another bond we have with each other is supporting our shared ministry.

DESIGNATED GIVING

We always tried to discourage it. The greatest amount of our budgets traditionally go to salaries and maintenance—neither of which are particularly exciting to a lot of people. But they have to be covered. One vestry member suggested we do a November in New York stewardship Sunday with no lights and no heat to show what would happen if we didn't cover those bases. We decided not to take her suggestion. But it would have made the point!

If some people are adamant about giving *only* for music, outreach, property maintenance, or some other pet interest, take the money. Rigidity won't make you any friends and it won't bring in the money.

At the same time, always emphasize the joy of giving. The Lord, after all, loves a cheerful giver.

QUESTION 39

HOW DO I INSPIRE
THE CONGREGATION
TO GREATER OUTREACH?

START WITH TEACHING

I come back to the World War II Archbishop of Canterbury William Temple's classic line: "The church is the only institution created to give itself away."

Consider the form and function of the local church as three actions of the Holy Spirit.

The Holy Spirit gathers
The Holy Spirit draws us into a particular fellowship of believers.

The Holy Spirit transforms
The words "transform" and "transformation" are unique to Christianity. Only the Spirit of God can truly transform a person—the inner working of grace.

Ideally, we come into a church and over time our lives are changed—changed for the good, transformed by his working within us and by the experience of worship, preaching, teaching, and fellowship.

Lonely ones of us find friends and support. Emotional needs are met. Those who need comforting find that comfort. We find answers to problems that plague us. We find, often unexpectedly, support in various aspects of life. We become more hopeful people. We know we no longer have to go it alone—we have the Lord and his people for support and encouragement.

We grow—in faith and understanding. Ideally, we catch a broader vision, are inspired and challenged to live less for ourselves and more for others. We discover that not only is the Lord a living presence, he also has a plan for us. That plan finds fruition in the third step.

The Holy Spirit sends

He sends us, strengthened by our transformational experience of prayer, worship, preaching, teaching, and community. He sends us forth into the ministry or ministries he has uniquely tailored each of us to carry out.

Thus, the term *outreach*. For some of us, it may mean ministry within the church. To others of us it may mean ministry outside—beyond our church to the hurting and needy of the greater community. For a lot of us, it's going to mean both.

Such going forth, moving out in our ministry, benefits us. We find our deepest satisfaction in doing the things the Lord has called us to do. That's where we experience life at its most abundant.

It's true we find our greatest blessing as we help others, as in different kinds of ways we address the myriad needs that exist all around us in the world. It's also the calling and function of our faith to help others. A generous spirit is a sign of godliness.

The Lord created us to be givers first. He's the original and ultimate Giver. He gave creation. He gave life. He gave his Son that by believing in him we might experience new and eternal life. He gave his Spirit to enable us to receive his wisdom for living and empower us to carry his love and caring to others.

To sum up the three-part action of the Holy Spirit as applied to the church, Michael Marshall wrote: 'The Holy Spirit is given to his church to renew and refresh it, but then to break it open. All gifts are given to be given away: not closeted and hoarded.'

Michael Marshall also wrote: "The church that lives to itself dies to itself."

SO HOW DO YOU MAKE IT HAPPEN?

How do you go about making a real difference in the lives of people outside your doors?

Start with two questions: *Who* needs help? *How* can we best help them? Some needs are already being adequately and competently met. They may need additional help you can provide. My priority was how to address needs that weren't being met.

The third question: What are our resources—financially and hands-on?

You can also expect that most people who've been involved with outreach have their personal preferences. Designated outreach interests are fine as long as you consider all the needs and options. We keep giving to them *only* because we've always given to them is not sufficient rationale.

When I first arrived as rector I organized a small mission study group, chaired by our deacon, to research (including site visiting) the various outreach organizations in our greater community. The group reported back to the Outreach Commission. From these reports—we weren't in a hurry, taking the better part of a year—the group made new and adjusted recommendations. To some organizations we pledged either financial or hands-on help. To others, both.

But we came to the culmination of our study with a renewed excitement and dedication—which we shared with the vestry and in a variety of ways the greater church.

My ordained ministry has always been with affluent churches. My biggest responsibility has been to make parishioners both aware of the needs in the community and willing to address them.

Your church may be smaller and less financially able to help. But there will be ways you can help, adjusted to your resources. It's not the magnitude, it's the depth of care and concern that matter.

When Jesus introduced his ministry by reading from Isaiah in his hometown synagogue, he explained his earthly mission: "The Spirit of the Lord is upon me, because he anointed me to preach good tidings to the poor; he has sent me to proclaim release to the captives, and recovery of sight to the blind, to set at liberty them that are bruised, to proclaim the acceptable year of the Lord" (Luke 4:16–24).

From that moment people were going to see Isaiah's promises realized in Jesus. The glorious promises of hope for the poor, release for the imprisoned, sight for the blind, freedom for the oppressed, the "year of the Lord" were being fulfilled: indicating that in this Jesus God's Spirit was on the scene at last and nothing would ever be the same again.

Jesus saw as his mission freeing, healing, and raising up the people life had held back, kept down, and hurt.

For him, the kingdom of God was both a spiritual connection with the Father and resultant concrete actions on our part. A king has subjects who make up his kingdom. That means we acknowledge him as our Lord and king. We seek to obey him by seeking his will and his guidance in putting his plan into practice. Part of his plan naturally applies to our personal destinies, the other to how we treat others. To love God with all our heart, soul, mind, and strength and to love our neighbor as ourselves means we also seek his guidance in loving others in concrete and practical ways.

The kingdom isn't the kingdom if it doesn't manifest itself in changed lives. That's how Jesus proved his mission to the doubters and unbelievers: by how he changed lives in concrete ways. That's what prompted Dr. Martin Luther King, Jr., to say: "Life's most persistent and urgent question is, what are you doing for others?"

Walter Rauschenbusch's ground-breaking *Christianity and the Social Crisis* over a hundred years ago startled the church of his time. It's hard for us to realize the revolutionary aspect of his work. We take church mission and outreach for granted. That was not the case in 1907, when his book was published. It sent a shockwave through the American church, became a national best-seller and brought Rauschenbusch international renown.

His great-grandson Paul Rauschenbusch in his 100th anniversary edition of the original work, entitled *Christianity and the Social Crisis in the 21st Century*, writes that his ancestor:

> identified the economic exploitation of the poor as nothing less than a national sin. As a pastor to the nation, Rauschenbusch preached both personal and societal repentance. He called upon Christians and the Church to lead the fight to redeem the nation through both personal and societal repentance. He called upon Christians and the Church to lead the fight to redeem the nation through both personal and national regeneration in accordance with the societal principles of Jesus.
> (San Francisco: HarperOne, 2009)

Our challenge today is the same as it was in 1907, as it was when Jesus began his ministry on earth. It is to redeem the soul of society. We know we'll never be able to do it by ourselves.

But with his help, as we open ourselves to the moving of his Spirit through us, his church, we can do all things.

QUESTION 40

SHOULD I ENCOURAGE SMALL GROUPS?

SMALL GROUPS CREATE CONNECTIONS

Opportunities like working together on projects can knock down barriers and pave the way for friendships. But the strongest, deepest ties are the kind of trust-building that can happen in small groups that meet regularly. There is no better way of building relationships among your parishioners.

Jesus and the Twelve were a small group. The Book of Acts shows the power and the mutuality derived from house churches. In a similar way, one of John Wesley's greatest contributions were the early Methodist societies that helped people grow as Christians and in love and service to each other and to the community.

The Anonymous Programs, adapting the Christian small-group mentality to helping people meet and overcome life-dominating problems, keeps proving every day, all over the world, the value of small groups.

Do your best to encourage, or launch if none exist when you arrive, small groups of some kind. Every church is different. But there are certain standard ingredients to every successful small group: Bible study or reflection, the opportunity to share openly, and—ideally—pray for each other.

The two most successful small groups at St. Matthew's are one for men only and one for both men and women. The mixed group meets on Wednesday morning, so most of the men who attend are either retired or work flexible hours. The format is Holy Communion, with prayer for each other and for others not present, usually led by the clergy in attendance, followed by Bible Study.

The men's group meets at 7:30 Saturday morning in the parish house. Here, too, the format stays the same. Gather for a very light breakfast, convene by singing a couple of hymns, then adjourn to round tables where one of the number introduced a topic of the day, followed by discussion and a closing prayer.

I've seen the relation- and trust-building power of these and other small groups I've been a part of through the years—starting long before I went to seminary.

Especially now, in our American culture of isolation, anger, and polarization the church needs both to model and benefit from small groups.

My small group historical and theological hero is John Wesley. He articulated with usual eloquence his fundamental belief in the communal aspect of Christianity.

According to Howard Snyder, Wesley once told a thoughtful questioner: "Sir, you wish to serve God and go to heaven? Remember that you cannot serve Him alone. You must therefore find companions or make them; the Bible knows nothing of solitary religion." Wesley put into action this advice for the next sixty years.

Snyder explains "When Wesley spoke of 'social holiness' and 'social Christianity,' he was pointing to New Testament koinonia. Christian fellowship meant, not merely corporate worship, but watching over one another in love, advising, exhorting, admonishing and praying with the brothers and sisters." (*The Radical Wesley and Patterns for Church Renewal*, Eugene, OR: Wipf & Stock, 1996, p. 148.)

It has been said that John Wesley and his movement, later referred to as Methodism, for his insistence on the methodical coming together of Christians, helped save England from a revolution like the one in France.

Small groups had great power in the early church. They helped save England in the eighteenth century. I wonder what they might do for America in our time?

QUESTION 41

WHAT ARE PITFALLS TO AVOID?

DON'T LET YOURSELF GET INTO ANY PARISHIONER'S POCKET

Antiquated phrase. What's it mean? Another way to say it is, don't be beholden.

There's no gracious way to say this. But it's not a gracious concept: this age-old, deplorable tradition whereby some clergy, because they're clergy, feel entitled to free rides from parishioners.

I'm not talking about small Christmas gifts or dinners out or even an occasional entertainment or other evidence of appreciation.

I mean the big gifts, the ones that in our heart we know are too much.

This was introduced to me while I was still in seminary. In the fall of our senior year our class went on retreat. Our speaker was a renowned and sometimes controversial church leader, the retired presiding bishop of the Episcopal Church, John Hines.

Bishop Hines was a man of great personal charm, immense compassion for the needy of this world and a leader in the civil rights movement. He was also a man of iron principle.

His topic for us: "What I've learned in my forty years of ministry."

Bishop Hines touched on such unsurprising topics as "I wish I'd spent more time with my wife and family"; "I wish I'd learned earlier to pay less attention to the opinions of other people." I love this: "I recommend that at least once a week you submit to the exquisite anguish of reading at least one editorialist with whom you violently disagree." (I still haven't quite managed that one.) His reason? "It will help keep you mentally and emotionally malleable."

But the thing he said that made the greatest impact on me, that dug a groove that has stayed with me these thirty-plus years, is this: *"Never let yourself get into a parishioner's pocket. Because if you do, you won't be able to preach the gospel to that person."*

What Bishop Hines meant was that we must always feel free of personal entanglements that might in some way inhibit our ability to speak the words God wants us to give to his people—in sermons, teachings, and conversation.

I cringe when sometimes remembering the free houses I've turned down in delectable vacation locales. Yet I also know that when I stand up to preach and look my parishioners in the eye, I'm free.

DON'T NEED THE PEOPLE

This can be a tough one. We need the Lord; we don't need our parishioners, emotionally that is. Of course, we need them to work with us in carrying out our shared mission. We need them to support the cause of Christ. We need their willingness to volunteer their time, energy, commitment, and finances to building our church. They are the church, the local body of Christ.

We must not fall into the trap of needing strokes from them. They pay our way. How do we know we're doing a good job, except from their reactions and responses?

Yet we have to continually remind ourselves that we're here to serve, not please, them. Pleasing them will probably make them, and us, feel good. But this pleasing can become as addictive as Turkish Delight in The Chronicles of Narnia.

In the words of Adlai Stevenson: "Flattery is like smoke. It won't harm you unless you inhale it."

We, like King Saul, may begin to care more about the opinion of the people than we care about the opinion of God.

Yet it's God who has called us. He who is in the process of helping mold us into who we are yet to become. He whose plan of salvation, redemption, inspiration, and challenge he has called us to help him carry out.

And on the, hopefully, rare occasion when he asks us to advise an unpopular plan of action for the greater good, we need to be able to hear his voice more clearly than can the naysayers. Divine guidance is crucial. Like

Isaiah, we need to be able to hear the Lord's voice saying to us, "This is the way; walk ye in it." Whatever the people's reaction.

It's a thin line we must walk. The line between such engagement and caring that our people feel loved by us and the distance we need to maintain as a reminder to them (and to ourselves) that we are the Lord's vessel. We must never lose sight that first and foremost we represent *him*. Which makes us in some ways very vulnerable; subject to all kinds of transference issues.

From the time I landed my first parish job, I vowed I would never entirely believe either my good press or my bad. The same person who praises you to the skies one minute can cut you off at the knees the next—usually for reasons having nothing to do with you.

On the other hand, you will find among your people stalwart and loyal supporters who will support you no matter what. Some will go to battle to help you carry out the vision as you see it. Some will become friends for life.

But emotional and psychological dependence? No. Pray for the strength to avoid the trap.

DON'T TAKE YOURSELF TOO SERIOUSLY

Hard to avoid taking ourselves too seriously. We are, after all, on a holy mission. We are, empowered by God's Spirit, helping him build his church. And I am convinced, in agreement with Norman Vincent Peale, that the local church is the hope of the world.

These are serious times we're living in. We all know the church has lost its once prominent place in the culture. We know the so-called "Nones"— i.e., Gallup Poll responders who listed "none" as their religious affiliation outnumber us denominational Christians. Christian values, Christian traditions, Christian beliefs are under attack. The culture grows increasingly secular.

Who are we? Why are we here? What are we here to accomplish? What's our mission? These questions are more important for the church now that at any time in centuries.

Some would say that the church has lost its way—if not its reason for being, though we know that's not true.

So, in the light of all this, how do I get off telling you to not take it all seriously? Well, you must take your *call*, your *ministry*, your *mission* seriously. But don't take *yourself* too seriously. And remember: humility is the key.

QUESTION 42

WHAT ABOUT MY FAMILY?

REMEMBER THEY ARE YOUR FIRST PRIORITY

Years ago, when I was considering a move, I mentioned to a more experienced clergy colleague that I was worried about the possibility of moving my wife away from the area of the country she'd lived in for her whole life. How could I ask my wife, a native New Yorker, who loved her city and whose career was based in the town we currently lived in, to move to a whole other part of the country?

"Don't worry," my more experienced friend said, "God knows you have a wife. He cares about her, too."

My friend was right. Your spouse, your significant other, your children, whatever your family configuration, God loves them as much as he loves you and loves the church he's called you to.

Fortunately, our call took Nancy and me to a church near enough her roots and relational contacts to make the change a blessing for her, too.

There's also the matter of two-income families. Nancy had also had a successful career in our geographical area. As an interior decorator, she could have started over in a new locale, but since the new church was in a nearby town, she was able to keep the clients she had.

Having said that, sometimes clergy families have to make immense sacrifices in moves and other adjustments they would never on their own ask for. It's up to us to try to make sure they know we have some comprehension of what it's like for them. Tell them you get it. Tell them you know it's not easy being in their shoes in this new situation.

Though it can also be exciting and fun to be part of a new beginning in this wonderful place the Lord has called you all to.

When I became rector, some burdens that landed on my wife were unavoidable, but neither of us expected them.

In some ways, Nancy was uniquely suited to be a rector's wife. A lifelong Episcopalian, as an adult she'd been deeply involved in her local church. She'd served on the vestry, chaired committees, and grown close to the rector and his wife. She was even a licensed diocesan parish consultant to help churches conduct new rector searches.

All that wasn't preparation for the realities of what it takes to be a rector's wife. She wasn't, for example, quite prepared for the startling reality that I'd be working virtually every Saturday and Sunday. When other people were taking Saturday morning for family time I was heading for the office. For me, Saturday mornings were virtually always committee meetings or baptism and wedding planning.

As the wife of a small-town rector, she had more surprises. Like having a parishioner greet her in the grocery store with: "I know who you're having dinner with tonight!" Or the reality of suddenly having two careers: her own and that of being the rector's wife. Or sitting at dinner and having people pour out their stories and family concerns to her. Because by association she automatically assumed in their eyes a part of my pastoral identity.

And what about *her* identity? For a whole lot of people, at least at first (and not surprisingly), she was Terry's wife. That changed, of course, as she became known and valued by the community for herself.

You'll likely find that the time issue is the hardest for your family to deal with.

I can't remember how many times Nancy and I had planned a day off together when at the last minute I had to cancel our plans to do a funeral.

How many times I forgot to tell her I had a baptism or a wedding or wedding rehearsal and therefore couldn't do something she'd planned for us to do together, with our family or with our friends.

Please remember this: before you plan anything other than your regular work week, *check calendars with your spouse or partner.*

Finally, like it or not, there's no way you can possibly keep your family from being an extension of you to your church and community. One of our daughters, who lived in the same town and went to the same church I pastored, is married with children of her own. That puts her well beyond the traditional preacher's-kid stage. Even so, some of her friends would see her coming and start apologizing to her for not coming to church more.

Your family's stuck with your very public position. Do your best to understand what that can mean for them. Be as sensitive as you can to their needs. And, together, look for the joy of being part of the Lord's work in his church and in the community.

I once heard Bishop Robert Knisely of the Episcopal Diocese of Rhode Island say: "As clergy we have to keep a lot of balls in the air. Some of those balls are more fragile than others. The most fragile is your family."

QUESTION 43

WHAT IS MY SPOUSE/PARTNER'S OBLIGATION TO THE CHURCH?

NONE — WITH QUALIFICATIONS

The line, "They hired me, not my spouse" is true. Particularly in today's world, in which both members of a couple often have careers, your partner's career matters as much as yours.

Strictly speaking, no parish should expect your mate to contribute anything to your church, including attending services.

However, there can be a lot of exceptions, depending on the culture and traditions of your location.

Every wife of the rectors I understudied after ordination, and those I knew before, had clearly defined and very active roles in the churches their husbands led. Each set of activities was different, depending on the individual interests and talents of the women. All were strong, gifted personalities in their own right. Some were more front and center in parish life than others. All were visible and played an active role.

But I'm talking about leaders of affluent churches in the 1980s and before.

When in 1994 Nancy and I moved to Bedford and I became rector of St. Matthew's, old expectations of that still in many ways traditional community had eased. She was the first rector's wife to have a full-time career.

It's good to ask the search committee early on what the churches' expectations of the rector's spouse will be.

I did. They said, "None." But I knew the culture well enough to know that presence at worship and in at least some other ways was expected.

In her low key way, Nancy was present. And by the time we left, much valued and appreciated in her own right.

The location of the church can make a big difference. Some inner-city churches are less likely to have expectations of your spouse than some suburban and small town churches.

Ask the question. Learn the culture. Get someone you trust early on to tell you the truth. Are there expectations? If so, what are they? Which ones do your mate and you ignore at your peril?

Total honesty on both sides is not always easy to achieve when you're in the courting phase of a potential call. But it's essential so that you and your spouse or partner can both flourish in the new setting.

QUESTION 44

HOW DO I MAINTAIN THE CHURCH'S
AND MY ENERGY OVER THE LONG HAUL?

The length of my leadership of one church makes me an anomaly. Most senior clergy now stay for around five years.

Having said that, principles that apply to keeping energy alive for many years also apply to briefer ministries. To some degree these guidelines make sense for ministry in any church situation. The caveat applies to a church that is for some reason so sorely troubled or dysfunctional that it needs to take time out to address the negative issues at hand.

For the rest of us, I'm convinced any church leader can come up with practical ways of keeping their church lively and healthy.

A BUSY CHURCH IS A HAPPY CHURCH

A busy church is a happy church. Your people want to feel they're part of a church that is doing important, meaningful things, making a positive impact. Preach and teach church as adventure; all of us joined together in the greatest of all causes—to make the world a better place, to change the world for God.

REACH OUT

One project we tackled engaged the greater community in helping another local church rebuild their parish house. Called "Raise the Roof," members of our two congregations met to plan and then carry out a fund-raising campaign to the whole community, many of whom were members of neither or no congregation.

That we were successful beyond our expectations proved what can be accomplished when Christians work together to build and *be* the church.

To celebrate the successful conclusion of our campaign, we held a Raise the Roof celebration at our church. Everyone in both churches plus those from the greater community who had contributed were invited.

We began the evening with a joint worship service. The church was packed; standing-room only. The service featured what we called "dueling choirs." The choir from the benefitting church, massed in front of the altar on the main floor, would sing a gospel song. Then our choir, in the balcony, countered with a classical piece. Back and forth they went to the congregation's delight. After a few of these, we clergy said a few words to thank the Lord and everyone present for their help. We concluded with an exuberant congregational singing of "This Little Light of Mine."

After the service we adjourned outside to a dinner served under an enormous tent. The food was a joint effort, too: barbecue, greens, and corn bread that men and women from both churches had been working together all day to prepare.

Another initiative was aid to Gulf Coast victims of Hurricane Katrina. We made a call to our parishioners to bring necessities to the church parking lot. A team of volunteers packed the goods into two trucks driven by parishioners—one to Mississippi the other to Alabama.

We also helped rebuild the community center, a facility in the next town over where people could get food and clothing.

REACH IN

To the crucial ministry of mission outside our doors we also came up with ideas for keeping excitement and energy alive within our community.

One was our series of bicentennial events. The bicentennial of the consecration and dedication of St. Matthew's Church was 2010. Leading up to the bishop coming for a service of rededication in the fall of 2010, we held what we called "bicentennial celebrations," geared to re-engage parishioners with the long history of their church.

These events included a re-enactment of a Sunday morning service as it would have been conducted in the Federal Period. We used a 1796 Book of Common Prayer, which would have been in use at that time. We managed to rent period clothes for all the parishioners who attended. I preached a sermon as I playfully thought it might have been preached by the then rector.

One event we called "The John Jay Weekend." John Jay is considered the founding father of St. Matthew's. His retirement home is just a few miles up the road from the church. It was his idea to build the existing church to replace an earlier structure built in a nearby own. He loaned the church the purchase money. And he was the first senior warden.

We honored him at an event on a Saturday evening. A female parishioner and I, again dressed in clothes of the era, sat on a dais in the parish hall and read to each other from letters John and his wife Sally had written to each other.

Sunday morning featured John Jay's most recent biographer speaking both at the ten o'clock service and the coffee hour following.

Other bicentennial events were an old-fashioned Dinner on the Grounds. We had hay rides, apple-bobbing, pie-eating contests. Dinner was eating barbeque on the back field under a tent while being serenaded by a Bluegrass band.

Finally, we had an "Art and Architecture of St. Matthew's" weekend, with history-oriented tours of the Federal-era church and rectory, followed by a lecture describing the art and artifacts the church had accrued, mostly through bequests, over two hundred years.

The actual re-dedication of the church on Sunday morning two hundred years to the day after the original service, was the powerful culmination of all the educational and experiential activities that had led up to it.

Thanks to our church school's involvement, not just the adults but the children of every age had an idea of the historical meaning and importance of their church and the role they could play in the Lord's unfolding plan.

We found other reasons to celebrate through the years. One was the celebration of our parish house addition, which we did with the bishop and congregation following a bagpiper in joyful procession from the church across the lawn to the parish house.

Meet with your leaders. Encourage input. Ask them to come up with ideas they think can get your people engaged. Consider their talents and interests. Make the most of your church's unique history and other attributes. Be creative. Be Playful. Be willing to try anything that might strengthen the relational bonds of your people.

OUR ROLE AS LEADERS

Along with coming up with creative ideas for celebrating our church community, we need to regularly teach and preach what the church is in God's overall plan. This includes reminding parishioners that each of us is called to play our part in carrying out God's mission and plan. And if someone says, "I'm too old to volunteer," you can remind them they can still pray. Pray for our church, for the rest of us. Always teach the supreme value of every individual.

You can teach the meaning of the body of Christ and the importance of knowing and developing our spiritual gifts.

When Rick Warren's *The Purpose-Driven Church* came out I introduced his five purposes—plus two I added—first to the vestry then to the rest of the congregation in a Sunday morning sermon and via all-parish mailings.

Rick wrote that at Saddleback, the mega-Baptist church he pastors in Orange County, California, he'd come up with these five purposes of the church:

- Communicate God's message.
- Fellowship with other believers.
- Demonstrate God's love.
- Educate God's people.
- Celebrate God's presence.

Assuming that his "Demonstrate God's love" incorporated the crucial work of outreach and mission, I made these two additions to Rick Warren's original five:

- Stewardship of our resources and of the natural creation.
- Prayer.

Prayer, when inspired by the Holy Spirit, is the greatest power we have as Christians; the foundation for all we accomplish in his name.

QUESTION 45

WHAT WAS THE HARDEST THING YOU HAD TO DO AS A PASTOR?

BE WITH PEOPLE WHO HAVE LOST A CHILD

We know it's not natural to lose a child. In the general order of things, our children should outlive us. When they don't, no tragedy can compare with it.

I've been confronted with such awful grief situations several times in my ministry. On every occasion I've been flooded with grief for my precious parishioners who have lost their darling children. I've been starkly conscious of my complete inadequacy to help them in any way.

So what did I do?

I remember one loss of a child that was particularly brutal because it happened with no warning. It's bad enough when the child has been ill. A parent can never be prepared to lose a child. Such a loss is always traumatic. But losing a child in an accident carries heightened shock and trauma.

In this particular case, when the call came, I wasn't in the office. It was Friday, my day off. I was at home. It was a snowy winter morning. The phone rang. A parishioner told me he'd learned that a couple in the parish had just found out their son had been tragically killed in a highway accident.

I'll never forget going outside, walking Sophie, my Jack Russell Terrier, around and around in a big circle as the snow began to fall harder. And as I walked, I prayed. I prayed for the heart-broken family. I prayed the Lord would show me what I could do.

Which was, of course, nothing—except what I did. Which was to put my dog back in the house, get in the car, drive the short distance to the family's house, and—once there—hug them and sit with them.

Looking back, I don't think I said a word until it was time for me to leave. Words are useless at such times, attempts at verbal comfort a sham.

I prayed. I went. I hugged them. I sat with them.

Other situations have been different. Sometimes the Lord has given me words. This time he didn't. So I did all I could do. It wasn't enough. Nothing is enough at such times. But they knew I cared.

If such awful times come to you, I suggest you do what I did: pray. And trust the Lord to show you what is best for the situation. Surrender those moments to him, for the sake of the grieving family and for yours.

And I don't know about you, but the Lord has given me a unique love and caring for these bereft parents. No matter how much time passes, or whether I see them or not, they will always occupy a special place in my heart.

PART 5

PREACHING AND SERVICES

QUESTION 46

HOW DO I APPROACH PREACHING?

WITH FEAR, HUMILITY, AND PRAYER

We were having dinner at a parishioner's house. I was seated next to our hostess' sister, a sometime churchgoer who lived in another state.

At some point in the course of the meal she turned to me and said, "Do you like to preach?"

I said, "Preaching is one of the scariest things I do."

Obviously surprised by my answer, she asked, "Scary? Why?"

I told her. "Because who do I think I am to climb into that pulpit Sunday after Sunday and presume to speak the word of God to his people?"

If I don't have his help, I'm not going to preach anything worth hearing. Of course, as in every aspect of our ministry, the sermons we preach will be a mixture of us and the Holy Spirit. Flesh and Spirit inexorably intertwined.

But I pray always for more of him and less of me. I pray it for every part of my ministry. I pray it most intently for my preaching.

There is no higher calling, no greater honor, no comparable privilege, no more intimidating task than preaching.

Most important in our worship services are the manifest presence of the Lord and the word he has for us in the moment.

We must believe God is with us. Because if he isn't, we might as well go home. And I must believe he's giving me the words, at least inspiring the words I preach, or I might as well stay in my seat and never climb into the pulpit at all.

What I do is *pray*. I beseech him. There have been times when, feeling frustrated because the words weren't coming, I've cried out to him, "Lord give me your words for your people who are going to hear this sermon. You know what they need to hear, I don't. Give them what you want them to have."

They don't need *my* words.

They, we all, need *his* word. Our spirits crave his life-giving word. Without his word, our spirits wilt. But his word renews, refreshes, revives, instructs, and inspires. His word comforts us when we need comforting, challenges us when we need to be challenged.

His word commissions and strengthens us (in the words of The Book of Common Prayer) to do the work he has given us to do which is "to love and serve Him with gladness and singleness of heart." His word gives us the strength to go out and, with the help of his Spirit, make the world a better place.

You don't accomplish this with ho-hum sermons. It takes your passion and absolute commitment. You need to throw yourself, heart and soul, into the task and joy of preaching.

THE BEST PEACHING IS FRESH

It depends on revelation. "New every morning," is God's faithfulness. So is his word ever new. Alive. A teacher of mine said, "The Holy Spirit is always communicating."

Our prayer needs to be, "Lord, what would you say to us today?"

A dear old English minister we affectionately called Uncle Arthur once told me: "Give the people fresh bread. Fresh bread gives life. Stale bread breeds worms."

The living word brings life, because it comes to us from the heart and mind of God.

I will never preach a sermon as good as I think it should be. I keep praying the Lord will improve my preaching. I keep asking him to make me a conduit for his word to his people.

I want to be like the water hose in the hands of the Gardener, with fresh water flowing through me to nurture and nourish his word in the hearts and minds of his people.

STUDY PREACHERS AND PREACHING

You can find endless numbers of excellent books on the theology and practice of preaching. Read the ones that speak to you. Study what they have to say.

Read too many and you can get confused. When our youngest daughter was pregnant with her first child, her obstetrician told her: "In today's world, there are so many books on pregnancy, childbirth, and child-rearing, read too many and you'll end up overwhelmed and confused. Do your research. Stick with one or two and you'll be fine."

The same can be true of homiletics books.

I recommend studying the great preachers of the past. In the eighteenth century, Whitfield and Wesley. In the nineteenth, Spurgeon, Beecher, and Brooks. In the twentieth, James Stewart, Harry Emerson Fosdick, Gardiner Taylor, Billy Graham; many others. Look around today and see what popular preachers as diverse as Barbara Gardner Taylor and T. D. Jakes (*Time Magazine*'s "Best Preacher in America") are saying.

Why have these preachers kept vast crowds mesmerized? How have they lit a fire for Christ? How have they transformed cultures, changed lives, launched revivals?

Remember the storyteller. You may be more intellectual than emotional, more T than F on Meyers-Briggs. If you are, there will be people who are going to love your heady probing of the faith. But make sure you lighten the intellectual content with stories, a touch of humor, or something personal. It will give your listeners a break from the mental intensity of your message.

Meanwhile, if you're more on the F side, give the people enough practical and intellectual content to balance the heart. Our faith story is what we're called to share, explain, probe, and apply to the lives of our people. Storytelling requires lots of interaction. Whatever your personal preaching style, remember your audience. You may have a full manuscript, but know your sermon so well you can never be accused of seeming to read it.

DELIVERY

I've actually very occasionally seen preachers read their sermons, with little or no eye contact with the congregation. This sends two messages: one, I don't really believe what I'm saying because I'm glued to the page. Two, you're telling your listeners they really aren't all that important because you seem to be preaching to yourself.

Apply the Three E's: *energy*, *enthusiasm*, and *enjoyment*. They amount to good delivery. They can help you deliver less than your best message and still be effective. They tell the people: I believe what I'm saying. Because if it doesn't seem to matter to you, the preacher, it's not going to matter to them.

ALONG WITH THE GREAT PREACHERS, STUDY THE GREAT ORATORS, TOO

Winston Churchill, unparalleled for his ability to move people with his words, said about public speaking: "An effective talk is a series of facts all pointing in a common direction. The end appears in view before it is reached. The word anticipates the conclusion and the last words fall amidst a thunder of assent."

Wouldn't it be great to conclude your sermons to a thunder of assent?

Churchill also advised, counter to the old tradition of the three-point sermon, making only *one* point. He said no one can absorb or remember more than one point, anyway. We should feel good when they can do that! Churchill adds: "Of course, you can say the point in many different ways over and over again with different illustrations."

I also agree with this, though it doesn't always come naturally to me: "Vary the pose and vary the pitch. Finally, don't forget the pause." (James C. Hume, *The Wit & Wisdom of Winston Churchill*. New York: HarperCollins, 1994.)

Ah, the pause. There can be great power in the pause.

HUMILITY IS ESSENTIAL

Never, never, never get puffed up and prideful about your preaching. Hubris can be our chief stumbling block in every area of ministry, especially in preaching, because it's so public and because preaching is one of the primary draws or deterrents to church attendance. Remember: the Lord who provides the anointing can as easily withdraw it.

BE ENTERTAINING AS WELL AS ENLIGHTENING

A little entertainment isn't ungodly. Jesus' parables were all entertaining in some way. Humor can add a lot, too. As discussed, when we laugh we relax, we let down our resistance, we're more disposed to receive from the person who made us laugh—in this case, the preacher.

LEAVE THEM WANTING MORE NOT LESS

Finally, as in every good story, you want people to care about where you're taking them and what happens next.

I knew a rector once who would preach a fine sermon. I'd think, "Great sermon!" Then he'd proceed to preach a second. I'd think, "Not bad; a little long. But worthwhile." Then he'd launch into the third. By then I and the rest of the congregation were praying for him to end. By then we'd lost the energy to appreciate what had gone before. We just wanted out.

We never have to give them everything we have at one sitting. Again, consider Jesus' parables: never long, never boring, always leave them thinking.

STAY GOSPEL-CENTERED

You may use personal illustrations. But your sermons are not about you. You can tell the most powerful and moving stories of how people's lives have been touched, even changed. But your sermon is not, ultimately, about those people. You can astound and impress and clarify with theological musings. But your sermon is not about your impressions. Your sermon, every sermon, needs to be about *Jesus*—to finally and clearly point to him and bring his people to him.

PROPHETIC, NOT POLITICAL

There's a difference. When people ask me, "Do you preach politics?" I say, *no*. By that I mean that in sermons I don't specify individuals, such as the president or governor, or take political sides in the pulpit. In Bedford nobody but Nancy knew how I voted.

That's because I didn't want my political views and opinions to be a pastoral barrier between any parishioner and me. When I walk into a hospital room, I don't want the sick person to feel resistant to me because they know—and disagree with—my politics.

Some of my fellow clergy have taken issue with me. One man got angry, shouted, "Jesus would have preached about that." Would he? I'm not sure.

Certainly, Jesus did not ignore the evils of his culture. Neither do I.

He graphically and sometimes angrily called the religious establishment to account. And I've addressed issues of morality, equality, and the needs of the underprivileged. I've preached on the evils of racism; if you're a racist, you might call that political.

When lying seemed to be endemic in Washington, I preached on the importance of truth. When parents were caught paying bribes to private schools and colleges to help their children gain admittance, I preached on what an awful moral statement such behavior makes and what terrible values it teaches our children.

I preached on the shame of many high school students in the New York City area caught cheating on exams. Horrified by the unwillingness of our elected representatives to overcome political differences in order to help the greatest number of Americans, I preached a sermon titled, "What Would Jesus Say to the U.S. Congress?" I find this prophetic rather than overtly political. Confronted by the extreme polarization between liberals and conservatives, I called us to remember "*E pluribus Unum*," and cried, "I see plenty of *pluribus*. Show me some *Unum*." I've begged to see mutuality, wisdom, maturity in government.

I've preached on our responsibility as Christian Americans to do what we can to counteract the horrors of mass shootings. Political? Maybe. To me, prophetic.

Also prophetic, based on my reading of the Prophets, is that God has repeated his call to people to consider the idols of our lives and put God first.

You may be called to preach overtly political sermons. Sometimes it depends on where your church is located. I've read recently that in some urban areas churches are growing because they preach such social issues that some would call liberal views, just as I know that in some conservative areas of the country, conservative politics preached from the pulpit can be a draw.

But, I wonder, what about those people who might stay away from either approach because it doesn't coincide with their political views. And

I wonder about those others who might come if the gospel was preached—not overtly politically—but prophetically?

HOW DO YOU PREACH ON THE SPECIAL OCCASIONS? EASTER, CHRISTMAS, MAUNDY THURSDAY, GOOD FRIDAY

I TRY TO TAILOR THOSE SERMONS TO THE VERY DIFFERENT TRADITIONS AND EMOTIONS THEY ENGENDER

Easter

The hardest sermon for me to preach is on Easter Day. Easter is, of course, the centerpiece of our faith. If Jesus had stayed in the tomb there would be no church.

So how do you preach on this most crucial of days?

You can plan on certain conditions unique to Easter. The church will be full. A lot are Holly and Lily parishioners, to whom you mostly get to preach twice a year. You'll have out-of-town family and friends you've likely never seen before. You have the children. Depending on your Easter child care, some of them can be pretty little and pretty distracting. And don't forget that Easter is to some out there in the pews less about the meaning, worship, and spiritual power of the day and more about the new outfit, the Easter Egg Hunt, and the big family dinner they'll be having that afternoon.

The greatest celebration of the Christian Year. A real preacher's opportunity. Challenging, daunting, and, hopefully, fun.

How I've dealt with all these competing challenges in recent years is by combining the original event and characters—Jesus and his followers—with a contemporary take.

I've done this in recent years by starting the sermon introducing my-self as a radio broadcaster for the weekday "Morning in Jerusalem" show. This has enabled me to get the hard-to-get attention of some who have come prepared to be bored and planning in advance to tune out the sermon.

It also gives me the opportunity to include interviews with Mary Mag-dalene, John the Beloved, Peter, and others who witnessed the empty tomb.

One Easter while *Hamilton* was still new and the hottest Broadway show in years, I even included a rap song by one Josh Bar-Jonah. Yes, I learned to rap. You may think, "I'm not believing this." But nobody yawned, especially not the teens. Older people forgave me—or felt sorry for me!

Christmas

My theory is that people don't want theology on Christmas, they want magic.

In all the churches I've served, Christmas Eve is the Big Event, with Christmas Day reserved for elders who find it difficult to get out at night and to brave over-crowded services. We've also had newcomers, visitors, and unchurched who feel a need to be there on The Day.

Christmas Eve, as I mentioned above, I simply told The Story at the two earlier, iconic, services.

Our eleven p.m. was a Festival Eucharist, with major music and more pomp than our relatively low-church liturgy usually had.

For a sermon, every year I "became" a character at the creche. I en-joined the congregation to come back in time with me and imagine what it might have been like to actually be present on that night of nights when God entered the world as a baby.

I was a different character each year for twenty-three years. Starting with the obvious, historically accurate, characters of Joseph, a shepherd, a king (I finessed the timing), the innkeeper. One year I took a huge risk and "was" Mary; not, I realized, an easy character to channel, considering the fact of her giving birth.

Quickly running out of the actual players in the drama, I just made them up. Some years, more tailored to the whimsical, I was in turn a mouse, a rooster, a shepherd's dog, and the donkey.

Then I branched out. I became one by one a boy of the streets, a Ro-man spy, going from provincial inn to inn to spy out any potential attempts to overthrow the Roman regime. I was even, in the cocky taking of a dare, an inanimate object: I was for twelve minutes The Star of the East.

MAUNDY THURSDAY

Except for my preaching approach, the only two key liturgical events I completely changed after coming to St. Matthew's were Maundy Thursday and Good Friday.

Again, you will do what your theology, personal approach and style, and the traditions you've inherited indicate. Here's what I did:

Soon after arriving as rector I discovered that Maundy Thursday was pretty much a non-event. Not much energy, not much attention given, and not a lot of understanding on the parishioner's part of why it's so important.

So I began a teaching blitz weeks beforehand. I sent out an all-parish mailing explaining why Maundy Thursday is, second only to Christmas Eve, the most important night of the year for us.

I designed the evening: so-called Agape Supper in the parish house at seven p.m., featuring simple, meatless casseroles and my very brief teaching on how for Christians on that night Jesus and his disciples observed for them what would become the last Passover Seder and the first Eucharist.

At eight, the children went to an event planned for them in the church school rooms. I led the adults in silent procession from the parish house to the church. Then we went inside for a Communion service followed by The Stripping of the Altar, a dramatic service that left the church dark, with just enough light for people to find their way out, which they did in silence.

During the actual stripping, in the gathering darkness of lowered lights, one of our base soloists, in his powerful resonant voice, read from the balcony Psalm 22. Never had the words "My God, my God, why have you forsaken me?" seemed more heart-rending.

The sermon? Maundy Thursday presents a wealth of themes: the symbolism of fellowship at table; foot washing; the meaning of both Holy Communion and Passover and how Jesus was the ultimate sacrificial lamb; the betrayal of Judas; Jesus' agony in the garden (and how we all may go through our times of doubting God); the lesser betrayal (flesh not evil) that enabled the rest of the disciples to sleep even when Jesus begged them to stay and watch with him. There are plenty more options. Sermonic riches abound.

GOOD FRIDAY

The other service I changed completely was Good Friday. You will observe Good Friday according to the tradition you've walked into and your own personal understanding of our Lord's passion.

For a variety of reasons, I stopped the traditional three-hour service and substituted one that lasted an hour.

We packed a lot into that hour. It was a modified Stations of the Cross. We did seven, and instead of walking around the church, they were indicated verbally. The service was conducted by my two clergy assistants and me. You could as easily use lay readers.

We began with a hymn, followed by a short Bible reading explaining the first station. Then I gave a short meditation, followed by a brief period of silence, followed by a prayer by the second reader, followed by music from a soloist.

That was the format for the service: reading, meditation, silence, prayer, music.

I based my talks on characters at the cross: Pilate, Pilate's wife, Barnabas, Simon, who carried the cross, Mary the mother of Jesus, John the Beloved, Joseph of Arimathea. I branched out from these obvious characters and, with God's help, in twenty-three years I never did the same meditation twice. Thanks to the inspiration of the Holy Spirit.

Finally, for these and such other great liturgical moments as Epiphany, Pentecost, and All Saints we are blessed, as preachers and liturgists. We've been given untold spiritual depths and riches to mine as we are called—year after year—to preach once again the old yet ever-new story.

QUESTION 48

WHAT ABOUT BAPTISMS, WEDDINGS, AND FUNERALS

Someone once called us clergy "holy interlopers," because we're actually expected to be present at some of the most meaningful and intimate times in people's lives.

It's a remarkable privilege and an immense responsibility.

BAPTISMS

Baptisms and their preparation will vary in the details according to your denominational and local church traditions. Certain things hold true for all of us, though.

Preparation, for one. Whether you're baptizing an infant, a child of any age, or an adult, you need to meet with the key participants and teach them what baptism means.

You can explain that "One Lord, one faith, one baptism" means that if you're baptized once you do not need to be a second time should you change denominations."

Some of us "sprinkle," some tap the forehead with water three times, once for every name of the Holy Trinity. Some perform full immersion. I have all three in my family tradition. We're equally baptized, whatever the form. All it takes to be efficacious is water and the Triune name. I always tell the laity that though baptism is considered a sacrament by some of us and not by others, they as lay people can also perform the service.

In my preparation teaching I explain the theology of baptism and the ancient traditions—starting with the baptisms for the cleansing of sin conducted by John the Baptist and ancient Jewish sects like the Essenes.

I talk about the sin nature we're born with and how baptism washes us clean of Sin, capital "S," though as human we naturally continue committing sins, lower case "s." Thus our need for ongoing repentance leading to forgiveness.

I explain the story of the baptism in the early church, in which only adults were baptized, and then after a year of catechumen classes, culminating in group baptisms held once a year on Easter Eve. I tell how everyone first gathered outside the church building, lit bonfires, and re-told the story of God's plan of salvation.

Then just before midnight, the baptisms (all full immersion) were held in a pond or stream or, in some cases, in an indoor water tank. I describe how the existing Christians gathered on one side of the water, while the baptismal candidates stood on the other side stripped naked. This to symbolize casting off the old self. One by one they descended into the water, were immersed by the resident priest or bishop, then splashed out on the other side where they were immediately dressed in white robes to signify that they'd been washed clean and now shone with the light and the purity of Christ.

Following the baptisms, the entire group of Christians went into the church for the first Holy Eucharist of Easter.

At the service itself, I again more briefly explain the meaning of baptism and make the point that baptism is the most important event of our lives. Why? Because in baptism we are cleansed from Sin, reborn by the Holy Spirit, and in a spiritual sense made new. We also, through our baptism, now have membership in the body of Christ. We have become members of two families, our family of origin and the family of Christ, the church.

I usually read Mark's "Suffer the little children to come unto me" passage. And once the actual baptisms are complete, before the closing prayers, I walk infants around the church, to symbolize their membership in their new family, the church.

I've been fortunate; most babies tend to like me. Happily, for everyone concerned. There have been notable exceptions. One tiny boy spent the early part of the service purring with delight in his mother's arms. Then I took him, at which point he instantly began screaming bloody murder.

His face turned red with rage. His eyes bulged. The veins stood out in his forehead. He screamed the entire time I raced through the baptism. I thrust him back into his mother's arms, at which point he became once again the picture of righteousness, peace, and joy. The baby's daddy was my clergy assistant.

I always make a point of meeting the infant before the baptism. I may not take the spiffily-outfitted little mite in my arms. But I look him or her in the eye, chat them up, try to make them smile, whatever it takes for some initial bonding. My thought on this is that when I take the baby into my arms at the point of baptism, I'm not a total stranger.

The only other baby who hated me on sight, beside the one I mentioned above, was a baby girl who was held by her grandmother. I tried my usual charm routine; didn't work. The wee baptismal candidate, squirmed, looked the other way, actually went so far as to shake her head, no. No to this white-haired interloper.

Crest-fallen I turned away. Then I saw the baby was fascinated by a sizeable necklace the grandmother was wearing. The little one grabbed hold of it, giggling with delight. Idea!

I hurried back to the vesting room, grabbed the silver cross on a chain I normally wear only twice a year—Easter and Christmas Eve—put it on, came back to the baby, who reached for it happily. When the time came for me to take the baby, she reached for my chain, delighted.

There's a prayer in The Service of Holy Baptism in The Book of Common Prayer I like so much I've often prayed and then commented on it to the congregation.

The words that captivate me are: "Heavenly Father, we thank you that by water and the Holy Spirit you have bestowed upon *these* your *servants* the forgiveness of sin, and have raised *them* to the new life of grace. Sustain *them,* O Lord, in Your Holy Spirit. Give *them* an inquiring and discerning heart, the courage to will and to persevere, a spirit to know and to love You, and the gift of joy and wonder in all Your works. *Amen."* (The Book of Common Prayer, 1979, p. 308.)

An inquiring and discerning heart. The courage to will and to persevere. A spirit to know and love the Lord. The gift of joy and wonder in all his works. May we all maintain throughout our lives such positive attributes as these.

Here's a point for you if you've never held a baby before. It was never a problem for me, as my little brother was born when I was almost eleven, which meant I always got to take care of him and learned how to carry him as an infant. Which means I learned early on the baby fact that infants can't hold up their heads without help, because their neck muscles aren't yet sufficiently formed. So you have to make sure, when you take the baby, that the little head rests firmly on your arm or shoulder, so it doesn't—perish the thought—flop.

WEDDINGS

I love doing weddings. For me, it's one of the most fun things we do. And most meaningful. Weddings focus on the greatest force in the universe, love. The love the couple have for each other is a reminder to all of us in attendance that with love comes the promise of hope, happiness, and new beginnings.

There's more: weddings bring people together. Weddings are unifiers. You mostly don't know the other guests' opinions on politics or any other issues—because there are a lot of people present you've never seen before and will never see again. What you do know is that you're all there because you care about this couple and you want the best for them. The unifying power of weddings reminds me of what should be another, even greater and more powerful unifier: the church.

Get to know the couple

I usually meet with couples three times before the rehearsal. The first time is about getting acquainted, getting to know them, their past, something about their families, what's unique to their relationship, beginning with how they met. Every couple has the story of how they met, and they all love to tell it. I'm always surprised at how many times one and sometimes both members of a couple came away from their initial encounter with the thought: "That's the person I'm going to marry."

At the first meeting, I send them home with a questionnaire to fill out and bring to the second meeting. The questionnaire covers the bases: family background and relationships, adjustment to school at various stages of development, friends, sex education, dating patterns. It asks questions about finances, recreation, plans for children, religious background and expectations, and how they interact and communicate with each other.

As I tell the couple, these meetings are more for them than for me, a time out for them to think about what kind of marriage they want to create together. I also remind them that for most of us the marriage relationship we know best is our parents'. Do we want to reproduce it, adapt some but not all? Because in marriage and child-rearing, we're apt to unconsciously repeat what we've experienced, unless we stand back and with perspective make different choices.

In our second meeting we go over the questionnaire together. Usually, we sail through. There have been exceptions, though: conflicts emerge, frustrations, difficulties in some area of their relationship, with family, even how they spend recreational time. I'm frankly glad that if some issues exist, they feel safe in airing them. Some have required extra sessions. I met with one couple six times for reasons having to do with their families of origin. Twenty-five years later, they're still happily married.

Typically my third session with a couple has to do with two things: the actual service itself and wedding details.

First, I sit with the couple, each of us with The Book of Common Prayer in hand, and go through the wedding service line by line. It's important for the couple to know the theological and historical meaning of the service. And now is the time to do it. They certainly won't be aware at the rehearsal or the wedding. You can hope that in this quiet setting they'll get a deeper understanding of the deep importance of the commitment they're making.

Second, wedding details. Ask every question you can think of. How many attendants and guests?

Now is the time to make sure that the readings, and who will read them, are determined. Also see that they meet with the church organist to select the music, including hymns, if any.

Don't forget to ask if there will be any children—flower girl, ring-bearer—in the wedding party. This is important. I once did a wedding rehearsal in which everything went very smoothly, despite a plethora of attendants. No one thought to mention that there would also be seven little girls in the wedding. None were at the rehearsal. My first clue was when I looked down the aisle to see the bride starting down the aisle on her father's arm and preceded by a little covey of lovely little girls, some of whom were joyfully flinging petals. The problem was that no one had thought to make a plan for what to do with the little mites once they made it to the altar. They weren't noisy. They were fidgety, therefore mildly distracting.

Guests love seeing the little kids come down the aisle. People chuckle. It breaks the tension. But you need to make a plan at the rehearsal for what to do with them once they've arrived. If they're too young to stand quietly at the service, determine who can nab them and hold them in a pew.

Photographers

Some can be difficult. I meet with photographers before the service, explaining to them—as I have earlier to the bride and groom—that since this is a religious service, we can't have the photographers, flash or no flash, providing distraction during the service. They can be in the balcony a la the royal weddings, or standing mostly out of view on the side, not back and forth between the wedding party and the guests, which I have actually seen. I permit photographers, with flash, to stand in the front to get the bride and groom coming up the aisle and, at the end of the service, going back out. But they have to mostly disappear during the ceremony.

One photographer disagreed with my edict so vehemently he almost punched me. I was explaining to him my guidelines. He said, "No. You're wrong. The photographs are the most important thing. I'll do whatever I have to do to get the best shots."

I told him otherwise. It got pretty heated. I held my ground. He submitted. Grudgingly.

Another photographer agreed to everything I said, then mid-ceremony came running down the aisle, bulb flashing. I ignored him. I've seen some clergy when confronted with this stop the service and dress down the photographer. I wouldn't do that. Better to ignore them and focus on the couple. Why emphasize the distraction?

Other details

Will they have a receiving line? Important to determine in advance. Any special seating requirements for family or friends? Make sure the couple meets with the organist or has a plan for any special musicians or a soloist. The near-perfection they long to achieve depends on the details. Will they have a receiving line—if yes, where will it be? Who will be part of it?

Rehearsal

Once the couple, their attendants and parents, readers, and any other participants have gathered, I get everyone's attention, and seat the mother of the bride and the groom's parents in their allotted front row seats.

Then we line up the male and female attendants as they'll be at the wedding. Some will have this planned in advance. Others won't. I have the father of the bride, or other presenter, standing between the bride and groom, face to face with me, until the point in the service—which I now go through in brief—when he makes the presentation and sits down.

Make sure you have the groom and the attendants, once they've come to the front, turn so they can watch the bride come down the aisle. But I always have them practice, once the bride and her presenter have stopped in front of me, turning in to face the couple. I usually go over it more than once. They need to make the turn smoothly, as one. Good choreography makes for good liturgy.

I learned to do this because of a wedding I saw years ago during which the attendants, once they'd arrived at the altar, remained facing the guests in the pews, rather than of the bride and groom. Distracting.

Having talked through the service, giving the couple the opportunity to practice their speaking parts, I have everybody go back to the front and then we practice marching in. Don't walk too fast. We're not in a hurry. No bunching up. Leave plenty of space between the attendants. The same is true at the end of the service. I actually keep a hand on the shoulders of the groomsmen who, once the bride and groom have recessed out, present their arm to a bridesmaid and wait for my "Okay" before going out.

Having covered the service and processional and recessional, I get everybody back in front to ask if there are any questions. There always are.

Preach a homily

Don't talk long, but also don't miss this opportunity to talk about Christian marriage, the lived-out sacrament we pray this marriage will be.

Small Weddings

Not all weddings are as elaborate (and therefore complex) as I've indicated above. Some couples choose to have small weddings—family and closest friends or family only. This has been especially true during the pandemic. I rehearsed one wedding (no guests, couple only) by phone from Rhode Island. They were in Alaska!

FUNERALS AND MEMORIAL SERVICES

When it comes to times of loss, my prayer is: "Lord, help me be appropriate."

Just as we are all so different, so we all grieve differently. A pastoral approach that helps some may well not help others. That's why psychological studies show that couples who have lost a child often have major problems in their marriage. Because one may well feel the other is not showing proper grief, when actually they handle pain in different ways.

So I pray. And hope I'm providing some comfort.

It helps when you've been in a church for a long time, as I was. Then you've built up in-depth relationships through the years. You know the people. They trust you. Even then, some losses, like that of a child, are so grievous you're left speechless with sympathy and hurt for these people you love so much. And sometimes being speechless is appropriate. Usually they don't need your words. What can you say, anyway? The last thing people need, or want, are truisms. Spare me platitudes. They help some people, but they won't hear them from me.

Usually just being there is enough; the old seminary phrase: "ministry of presence." Pray, trust God to give you what you need to be helpful in the moment.

When it comes to the service, I let mourners have whatever they want. I've seen clergy and even organists say things like, "We don't do that."

I have never said no. The funeral or memorial service isn't about me. The Prayer Book gives us the liturgy. My sermon gives me my chance to make the human and theological points I consider important. If someone should ask for something outlandish or vulgar, I'd steer them. But in all my years of ministry that's never happened.

I also allow as many remembrances as the family want. Almost always, they're as concerned as I am that the service not run too long; the service is painful enough for them as it is.

On the other hand, when they have a need to express their deepest feelings in remembering their loved ones, I don't stop them. I've heard clergy say, "Keep it to two or three minutes." You won't hear that from me. In the face of untold anguish, who am I to draw arbitrary lines? With friends, maybe, if there are an unwieldy number of speakers. With family, never. Now is their chance to remember, their chance to celebrate, their chance to express thoughts, feelings, and emotions of love and loss they may never have the forum for again.

I do tailor the length of my remarks to the length of the service. My homiletical goals are first, to recall the personal attributes of the person we've gathered to celebrate and, second, make the gospel points—that the Lord who created and gave his life for this loved one has prepared for him or her a new, eternal life that is beyond anything we can imagine in this realm, a life unspeakable and full of glory. These are my themes—always expanded and tailored to the personality of the person we've lost, to the family and friends at the service, and the need always to point to the Lord— the author and finisher of our faith.

A FINAL NOTE: some clergy refuse to do baptisms, weddings, funerals, or memorial services for anyone not a so-called "Member in good standing." I've never understood this. If we say no, are we doing it out of some need for control? As somebody said, "We're ordained to administer sacraments, not our own agenda."

I'll perform pastoral services for anyone who asks; members or not. They may be un-churched, or have been turned away from the church they feel is theirs for the "good standing" or some other rule.

Not me. Who am I to refuse the services of the church to anyone? Would Jesus have made sure people had listened to some prescribed number of his teachings before he'd pray for them?

Also consider this: people who don't know you or your church come to you, get to know you, feel welcomed and at home, and when they have a pastoral need or decide they want to join a church, they're apt to come back. Evangelism.

DO THE SEASONS OF THE CHURCH YEAR MAKE A DIFFERENCE?

FOR LITURGICAL DENOMINATIONS, THEY SHOULD

I realize that we don't all give equal emphasis to the seasons.

When I was growing up in the Congregational Church, we celebrated Christmas, Easter, and—in Holy Week—Maundy Thursday and Good Friday. I didn't know the term liturgical seasons. We had no seasonal colors. The clergy didn't wear stoles. Worship garb consisted of a black robe. This austere approach to worship dominated Anglicanism for the four hundred years from the English Reformation until the medieval revival of the Oxford Movement.

Nothing wrong with simplicity. It has its purpose: nothing to distract from the primacy of the preaching of the word. I honor my religious roots and traditions. I understand them. I'll always be grateful for the foundation they gave me. It's up to you, or course to value, teach, and lead your church in its tradition.

What initially drew me into the Episcopal Church was the more interactive liturgy, The Book of Common Prayer, and the recurring drama of the liturgical seasons.

The whole year, from its beginning on the First Sunday in Advent to its close at the end of November, gives us the Ignatian opportunity to re-live the Lord's life with him.

Every time we journey around the Church Year mountain again, hopefully we deepen our understanding of who the Lord is and can be to us. Hopefully, as with the bride and her beloved in The Song of

Solomon, our love relationship with Jesus grows deeper, sweeter, and more transformational.

As a rector, one of the major seasonal differences I decided to emphasize was between Advent from Lent.

There are similarities, of course. Both are times of preparation—preparing ourselves to celebrate our two greatest festivals. Both are times for self-examination and renewed commitment.

Both are about kingship. Advent points to the *coming* King who is entering his world to save and ultimately establish his reign over it. Advent culminates in Christmas—the baby King born to a virgin and laid in a manger. It's also about preparation—getting ready for the child's arrival.

Lent also reminds us of our King—come to die for us then rise from the dead, King over death, King of the universe!

In Lent, like our Lord, we are drawn into a place of examination. The length of time—forty days—is the same as his sojourn in the wilderness. Forty comes from the ancient Hebrew number for testing. Lent is our annual opportunity to take time out, find some space for reflection, and, with his help, prepare ourselves for his passion and ultimate triumph.

There are also marked differences between the two. Advent is about joyful expectation, anticipation, the excitement of a family preparing for a birth. Lent is necessarily about repentance, cleansing, opening ourselves to receive the great gifts of salvation and eternal life. Lent is thoughtful, reflection.

Advent ideally features *some* quiet reflection. But it's also about getting ready. Think of the excitement of painting the nursery, buying baby clothes, all the baby paraphernalia. When you do that, for me all the running around getting ready for Christmas doesn't seem so onerous. Instead of decrying the commercialization of Christmas, which I can't do anything about anyway, I've decided to see all the busyness as less a distraction and more a metaphor for preparing to celebrate the Lord's arrival into our lives. After all, even non-believers wouldn't be buying presents and partying if Jesus hadn't been born.

With that in mind, when as rector I had the chance, I replaced our church's traditional purple Advent hangings with blue.

Purple as the color of kingship applies to both seasons. But for me, purple is more serious than blue. Blue seems lighter, happier, more in keeping with a baby. Purple seems heavier, makes a more authoritarian statement than gentle blue.

Before I authorized the new blue hangings, I did some research and discovered the Sarum rite of the liturgically spontaneous Middle Ages was blue. That's all the backup needed. Purple for Lent. Blue for Advent.

QUESTION 50

HOW CAN I MAKE
THE SEASONS DISTINCTIVE?

**SEE EACH SEASON AS AN OPPORTUNITY FOR TEACHING,
ENGAGEMENT, AND CELEBRATION**

Teaching

The cycle of the Church Year gives us another great opportunity for teaching. Teach the biblical foundation. Teach the meaning of our denomination's liturgical traditions that have accrued around each season. Teach the impact the seasons can have for us as Christians, not only biblically, historically, and liturgically but also in our individual lives. How do we benefit in our spiritual journeys from our annual observance of the Christian Calendar?

Engagement

The seasons provide us with a wonderful opportunity to overcome boredom. With the exception of Pentecost, the length of which makes sense in some ways and in others feels extreme, all the seasons are short enough to maintain the corporate energy.

We need to make the most of the meaning while exaggerating the differences of each season. Find the key word or phrase and build on it.

Examples:

ADVENT: hope, anticipation, expectation, birth, parenting, humility, God-given ministries (as in God's call to Mary and Joseph).

CHRISTMAS: joy, our calling, kingship, glory, trust in God's protection (as he protected the babe from Herod's threat), God's trust in us (as he was willing to entrust his Son to be born a defenseless baby to a poor human mother).

EPIPHANY: "going forth," in this case going forth to carry light—the light of Christ. The three kings were forever changed by the light of God shining forth from the baby in the manger. Transformed, they went out, out from the holy scene in the stable and forth to carry the light into the darkness of the world. So are we called to be his light-bearers in our individual lives and communities. Adventure. Seeing our individual spiritual journeys as great adventures reminds us of the adventurous route the wise men took in searching for the baby. Persistence (the wise men studied for many years to determine the birth date, so should we persist in our search to know him better). Humility, as in our need for humility, based on the wise men's kneeling in the muck of a stable floor to worship a peasant child.

LENT: start by making the most of Ash Wednesday. The Book of Common Prayer gives us Episcopalians a very effective Ash Wednesday liturgy. It's a powerful call to self-examination, repentance, prayer, self-denial, and meditation on biblical texts. I wasn't less moved as a boy, by our Ash Wednesday observance as Congregationalists.

We can continue through Lent using these as themes for sermons and teachings. Other Lenten topics include: giving; prayer; listening—to the Lord, our friends and family, our unconscious. What it means to be open— open to the Lord, open to others, open to the wisdom of the created order. And pride—as in, how it separates us from God, and from other people.

HOLY WEEK

One example of how to engage parishioners in a special liturgy is Palm Sunday.

Palm Sunday has the potential to be one of the single most liturgically dramatic days of the Church Year. From beginning with joy and celebration at the beginning of the service to mournful anticipation of our Lord's death at the end.

In keeping with that, I recommend starting the service outdoors (weather permitting), with brief prayers and Scripture reading, then marching in procession—choir and clergy followed by the parishioners—into church.

It's beneficial to have, if you can, a musician head the procession. I've been in churches with bagpipes leading us. I love the pipes, and have used them a lot for various services and ceremonies. But for the early spring morning of Palm Sunday, I prefer the playing of a single lute or flute: light, bright, evocative. Our lute-player stationed immediately behind the crucifer, led the procession. Then came the choir, clergy, and parishioners.

Once inside the church, the lute-player stationed herself at the front and continued playing until everyone was inside. When everyone had settled in, our organist thundered out the opening bars of "All Glory, Laud and Honor." Joy. Hope. Triumph. But for only a few minutes.

The passion provides the transition from Palm Sunday to Good Friday. We tried various ways of presenting the passion—from acting it out with characters in full costume to the simple reading by my two clergy associates and me.

Always, we sang "Were you there?" as our concluding hymn and left the church in solemn silence.

PENTECOST: The Holy Spirit (the active manifestation of the Trinity, ever present with us here, in this realm); power for living; God's wisdom and guidance; the early church as described in the Book of Acts; the meaning of church; what it means to be a Christian; how we're called to carry on the ministry of Jesus in our lives and times.

As we come to understand the meaning, power, and potential impact the seasons of the Church Year can have on us as individuals and corporately, as the local church, they become increasingly important to us.

Observing the special days and seasons not only draws us closer to each other but also closer to the God who makes himself known to us year by year in our walk with him. And as we live our lives based on this understanding, we move closer to fulfilling the purpose he has for us.

WHAT ABOUT PREACHING ON NATIONAL HOLIDAYS?

THANKSGIVING

This day is made for preaching. As a holiday, it unites our faith and our patriotism. It reminds us that as Christians we are citizens of two nations—the United States and the kingdom of God. Our call and challenge is to be good citizens of both. As rector I designed a service that speaks to this dual nationality.

Borrowing from John Harper, my rector at "The Church of the Presidents," St. John's Lafayette Square in Washington, DC, I called our St. Matthew's service the "Harvest Festival Service." Held at ten o'clock Thanksgiving morning, I chose Thanksgiving prayers from The Book of Common Prayer and featured a lot of congregational singing. Which the people enjoyed, because all the hymns were familiar:

Come, ye thankful people," (St. George's, Windsor); "We gather together" (Kremser); "Now thank we all our God," (nun danket alle Gott); and "For the Beauty of the Earth." Ideally you will choose favorites familiar to your church.

For Scripture texts, through the years I stuck with Deuteronomy 8:1–3, 6–10, and Psalm 33.

Preaching on Thanksgiving was my delight! Looking back, I recall a sermon based on the lesson from Deuteronomy. As we used to say in seminary, "This will preach!"

Here in Deuteronomy the preacher is reminding the people of everything God has done for them in past times. He brought them out of slavery in Egypt. He took incredible care of them for forty yeas in the wilderness.

For forty years, he fed them, he sheltered them. For forty years, miraculously, they wore the same clothes and the same shoes—and they never wore out! That's because God took care of them. He performed miracle after miracle to make sure they would be all right. Because they were his people. They belonged to him.

Now Moses, the old-time preacher, is worried. He's concerned that the people, because they can now buy their own food and clothes and provide for shelter for themselves are going to forget the essential truth. Which is that all good things come from God.

The remaining thrust of my message was my hope that all of us gathered that day, unlike the wayward Hebrews, not forget.

I recall others through the years. Such as: "The Power of Thanksgiving," in which, using the line "God inhabits the praises of his people," from Psalm 22:3, I stressed the supreme value, and potential power, we find in thanking and praising God—and the importance of thanking other people.

Thanksgiving Day stories from my own life, poignant and for me life-enhancing, came into play. And, back to stories, I had wonderful times making up characters—one an indigenous American boy—who might have been present at the first Thanksgiving.

I also did several American history snapshot sermons, emphasizing times in our nation's past—such as the first Thanksgiving after the Second World War ended—when we had unusually meaningful reasons for thanking the Lord for his help and deliverance.

FOURTH OF JULY

Most people in your church will want to sing patriotic hymns and hear patriotic sermons for this service—the Sunday closest to Independence Day.

For me, it's been, hopefully, a balance between flag-waving and a call to prayer, often for repentance, for our nation.

In the desperate time of the first summer of the pandemic, I preached a quick overview of the great moments in our national history, while not ignoring the desperate need for racial justice. Pandemic, racial inequality, for so many financial desperation—too much, daunting for this or any preacher. All you can do in such a time as that is throw yourself on God's mercy and implore him to give you his words for his people.

MEMORIAL DAY

Memorial Day was an opportunity for more patriotic hymns, with an emphasis on sacrifice—with thanks to our veterans through the over two hundred years of their service.

One Memorial Weekend Sunday I had the unique opportunity of preaching about the origin and scriptural basis of "The Battle Hymn of the Republic," emphasizing the song's history and author, Harriett Ward Beecher. It was made more special for us because she had once, in great old age, worshipped at St. Matthew's.

Memorial Day also lends itself to the preaching theme of sacrifice generally. The Bible abounds with rich stories of saints in both the Old and New Testaments who sacrificed to further the cause of God. We can bring sacrifice home to our parishioners as we talk about what parents sacrifice in raising their children and how various people in various walks of life make daily sacrifice for others and for the common good. In every close relationship, we're all going to be called to make sacrifices in some ways. Preach the need for sacrifice, but also the joys of sacrifice.

A PARISHIONER HAS ASKED ME TO DRIVE EVIL SPIRITS FROM THEIR HOME. HOW SHOULD I RESPOND?

STUDY THE SITUATION

Meet with those who've made the request. Find out from them why they feel their house needs spiritual cleansing. Try to discern if it's truly the presence of evil or some relational conflict that's causing unusual anger or resentment within the family system. If the latter, try to encourage the person or persons to seek counseling.

But if you feel they make the case for the existence of some evil presence in their home, determine the best way to help them. Whatever you do, don't try to brush off their concerns or indicate that there is no such thing as evil spirits. Exorcisms, of people or places, was standard practice in New Testament times. Jesus and the disciples delivered people of demons as regularly as they healed them physically.

Before going further it's important to consider the biblical understanding of how we can battle the forces of evil in our lives and ministries.

THE WAR AGAINST EVIL: A BIBLICAL OVERVIEW

Paul, in Ephesians, describes God's people in various terms: we are a legislative assembly, a family, a temple, and the bride of Christ. All these seem reasonable. Then Paul makes what seems to me, since I first came to understand it's meaning, an astonishing statement. The final picture Paul paints of God's people is that of an *army*.

Us? An army? According to the Apostle, yes. Read this in Ephesians 6:10–12:

> For we are not fighting against people made of flesh and blood, but against persons without bodies—the evil rulers of the unseen world, those mighty satanic beings and great evil princes of darkness who rule this world; and against huge numbers of wicked spirits in the spirit world.

If you've been raised and educated in the mainline church as I was, you may well have grown up with little or no knowledge of Satan or evil. I was told as a child, "There's no such thing as the devil."

And so I believed until I was in my early thirties. Then, after a powerful, life-changing experience with the Lord that altered the course of my life, I became part of a charismatic renewal church. It was the 1970s. Charismatic renewal, which began with an Episcopal rector, Dennis Bennett, in Seattle was making inroads into various denominations in those days.

With the renewal came a renewed understanding of the ministry of the Holy Spirit, including the manifestation of spiritual gifts, and a more literal understanding of certain New Testament teachings, such as the power and presence and action of embodied evil.

Whereas traditionally exorcism had been mostly confined to the Pentecostal churches and, in the Roman Catholic Church, to certain priests especially trained and set apart for the task, it now became standard practice in certain charismatic circles.

I was present at several exorcisms. I've seen the manifestations of evil before and during the exorcisms and the marked changes in the men and women who'd been delivered.

Having witnessed these deliverances, I went back to the Bible to see what it had to say about evil and the war we've been called to wage.

Paul writes: "For though we walk in the flesh, we do not war according to the flesh, for the weapons of our warfare are not of the flesh" (2 Corinthians 10:4).

Our primary weapon, it turns out, is prayer.

WHAT PRAYERS DO I PRAY?

Here's a prayer from "Celebration for a Home," from *The Book of Occasional Services*, published by The Church Hymnal Corporation of the Episcopal

Church, 1979. (This book is suitable for use in any denomination, but yours may also have specific exorcism program, and other resources.)

> Let the mighty power of the Holy God be present in this place to banish from it every unclean spirit, to cleanse it from every residue of evil, and to make it a secure habitation for those who dwell in it; in the Name of Jesus Christ our Lord. *Amen.* (p. 132)

If the residents of the home indicate a particular room or place in the house where they've felt the presence of evil, go to that spot. Pray directly. Address the evil one.

Pray like this:

> Satan, in the name of Jesus, I claim the victory over you. I command you to loose your hold on this place and on those who call it home. In Jesus name, leave. Go from this place and never return. This house belongs to Jesus. This place and all its inhabitants are covered by the blood of Jesus, the blood of the Lamb. You have no place here. Go and never return.

Then I pray the following:

> Father God, in Jesus' name, I claim this house for you. Drive out all evil and fill it with your Spirit. Consecrate it by the presence of your Spirit so that all who live here and all who enter will feel your holy presence. In Jesus' name—*Amen.*

You'll notice my use of *the Lord's name.* Over and over in the New Testament you see the power of Jesus' name used by the disciples in conquering all kinds of evil. I've learned through experience the power you and I and all Christians possess in the name of Jesus.

I saw the astonishing power of Jesus' name in action when I was serving in the church in inner city Baltimore.

One weekday morning Sid Rigell, the pastor, and I were in the thrift shop attached to the church. Suddenly the door burst open and a man obviously shot up on drugs, filthy, and disheveled staggered in. He lunged at Sid and, to my horror, I saw he was holding a knife.

The man growled, "I'm gonna' kill you, preacher." Sid was roughly a third the height and weight of his attacker. Before I could move, Sid shouted. He cried out a single word: "Jesus!"

Immediately, the man dropped the knife, sobbed, "I love God, I love Jesus," turned and ran out the door.

The name of Jesus!

For a more in-depth understanding of deliverance from evil, I suggest reading *Deliverance from Evil Spirits: A Practical Manual*, by Dr. Francis MacNutty (Jacksonville, FL: Christian Healing Ministries, 1995).

A final thought on the battle to overcome evil. It is crucial for us to remember that we must not fear Satan or his forces. We are assured of ultimate victory.

How is that? Because the Bible is very clear on this point. In Colossians 2:13-15, Paul writes:

> When you were dead in your sins and in the uncircumcision of your sinful nature, God made you alive with Christ. He forgave us all our sins, having canceled the written code, with its regulations, that was against us and that stood opposed to us; he took it away, nailing it to the cross. And *having disarmed the powers and authorities, he made a public spectacle of them, triumphing over them by the cross.* (NIV)

Christ has *already defeated* Satan and his powers once and for all. He did that by his death on the cross and by his resurrection. He won the ultimate battle for us.

That's why when we pray against the wiles of the evil one, he must go. In the name of Jesus and the authority that comes with our redemption, we have the power over all evil. But we do have to claim the victory and exert it when the battle comes directly to us or someone we care for.

Concludes Paul: "But thanks be to God, who always leads us in His triumph in Christ, and manifests through us the sweet aroma of the knowledge of Him in every place" (2 Corinthians 2:14).

PART 6

LOOKING BACK / LOOKING FORWARD
THE CHURCH'S PLACE IN THE WORLD

QUESTION 53

LOOKING BACK:
HOW DID YOU MANAGE LEAVING?

EXTERNALLY, OKAY; INTERNALLY, NOT WELL

I knew the time was coming when I'd be forced to retire, due to the age restriction. In the Episcopal Church, you're ordained a priest for life. But you can no longer serve as rector after the age of seventy-two. As it was, my bishop gave me a two-year extension.

The parishioners and I knew for way too long that the time was coming when I'd have to leave. I stayed busy, wanted to give my all to the end. On my last day as rector, I took my associate, Rik Pike, to an area retirement home so he could meet, and thus begin to form pastoral relationships with, some of our people who lived there.

My last pastoral encounter as rector was with my oldest parishioner, ninety-nine-year-old Mina Edmonston. I gave Mina one last hug, got in my car, and began driving the hour-and-a-half trip to our house in Rhode Island. I was in such a fog, I got—briefly—lost on a road I knew well.

The fog lasted in one form or another for nearly three years. I was a classic case of a healthy, active professional forced into retirement.

I know what I'm sharing doesn't speak particularly well for my faith. But I had some of the classic thoughts—as in: Who am I now? I had the wonderful opportunity of returning to Christ Church Greenwich where I'd served as associate rector before coming to Bedford. But that was part time. I'd have no responsibility there. What would I do? Would anybody respect me now, or was I just like an old shoe, the classic old race horse, put out to pasture, forgotten, unnecessary, my best days over.

So the thoughts went. Not only did I miss my place, my role, my position, and my ministry as rector, I desperately missed the place and—most of all—the people of St. Matthew's. Sometimes I'd cry thinking of them.

My wife and children were worried. They sent me to a neurologist. Was there something physically wrong with me? I took all the tests. I scored just fine cognitively and physically—nothing wrong with me, cognitively or physically that is.

Then as I was leaving, the young neurologist asked, "Have you had any major changes or upheavals in your life recently?"

When I told her, she said, "Oh, that's what it is: you're depressed."

I'd never been depressed, had no idea what it felt like, certainly didn't recognize the symptoms in myself.

The knowledge didn't make me feel any better, but I think it gave my family some relief, though they—and close friends—still saw me for a long time as not myself.

I had to come through the grieving process. Apart from the love and support of my wife and family, I threw myself on the mercy of God. One of my symptoms was not being able to concentrate very well. Another was an uncharacteristic lack of initiative.

I went to my long-time place of refuge, the Psalms. Among other uplifting verses and other psalms, I clung to Psalm 18, to the words of David, the "man after God's heart," who when finally delivered from the hand of all his enemies and from the hand of Saul, exultantly cried:

> I love Thee, O LORD, my strength,
> The LORD is my rock and my fortress and my deliverer,
> My God, my rock, in whom I take refuge;
> My shield and the horn of my salvation, my stronghold.
> I call upon the LORD, who is worthy to be praised,
> And I am saved from my enemies.

David's passionate affirmation in one of his desperate times helped carry me through.

Three years have passed. I'm doing a whole lot better; no longer filled with gloom, no longer overcome with self-pity. I will always miss the people of St. Matthew's and what we had together. It tore my heart to leave them. Serving as their rector were the best years of my life. Up to now.

But I'm back energetically pursuing God, and his vision for the church in different ways and in different places. He, as always, has put me back on the path he has for me. Should you go through something similar in your life and ministry, look to him. Cry out to him for the help you need to overcome. He'll bring you through as has me.

QUESTION 54

WHAT WOULD YOU
HAVE DONE DIFFERENTLY?

IF I HAD MY TIME AS RECTOR TO LIVE OVER . . .

Echoing Bishop Hines, whom I quote above, I would have spent more time with my wife and family.

I would have taken more days off.

I would have worried less and trusted the Lord more.

QUESTION 55

IS THERE A CRISIS YOU FEEL
YOU AVERTED BY SOMETHING YOU DID?

I can't say whether it would have actually become a crisis for us at St. Matthew's or not. I'll never know for sure. What I do know is that what was a crisis for many other Episcopal churches, and dioceses, and that sent shock waves through the whole greater Anglican Communion, was not a crisis for us. Which may or may not have had something to do with the way I responded to this seismic event of the greater church.

Here's what happened. When Gene Robinson, a homosexual, was elected as the bishop of New Hampshire, the reaction in the parish was immediate.

One man made an appointment to see me, sat in my office and told me I needed to lead St. Matthew's out of the Episcopal Church. And I needed to do it now.

I told him I didn't think the situation warranted such an extreme measure. He left in a huff, but made no more mention of it—at least not to me.

I received several phone calls from other parishioners. One lauded the decision of the New Hampshire diocese. One echoed the negative reaction of the man who came to see me. The others were simply concerned and curious; how might this impact the church at large and St. Matthew's in particular?

The following Sunday, I took action. I didn't mention it in my sermon, but at announcement time, I took my Prayer Book and walked out toward the people in the pews.

I told them that since the sixteenth century, in the Church of England and carried over to us in America, we Anglicans had found our unity not in particular theological confessions, like the Presbyterians, or in edicts handed down by higher authority, like the Roman Catholics.

No. Our unity, I said, was not based in particular ways of looking at the faith, not in a theological belief system. In fact (attempt at a humor), I told them the Episcopal Church is a great place for rebels like me, who don't like to be told how to think.

Our unity, I said, has always been in this book: in The Book of Common Prayer. I said, "The word 'Common' in this case doesn't mean commonplace. It means *universal*. The church made the decision that our unity would be found not in our theology but *in our worship*. In other words, you could believe pretty much as you wanted, as long as you followed the forms of worship in the Prayer Book. The same is true for us Episcopalians today."

I went on to say that with that in mind, the election and ordination of a gay bishop in New Hampshire really had little bearing on how we at St. Matthew's lived out our lives as a community of Episcopalians in this place.

So why be exercised over it? Let New Hampshire do what they wanted. "Meanwhile," I said, "we're going to keep on doing what we do. Which is to love God and love and be there for other people—in our St. Matthew's community and in the greater community beyond our doors."

I talked about the joy of acceptance—accepting the differences of every human being, in Gene Robinson's case, the differences of hetero- and homosexuality. Actually, a minister's homosexuality has nothing to do with their competence as a vessel of God. The important question will always be: *is the person called by God?*

I felt, though didn't actually hear, a collective sigh of relief. I finished the announcements, one of which invited everyone to a coffee hour forum discussion immediately following the service.

There I introduced Chuck Banks, a lawyer who was both clerk of our vestry and vice chancellor of the Diocese of New York. I explained that Chuck would begin with an explanation of how the selection process for a new bishop takes place. Then, I said, he—and I—would welcome any questions.

I thought there might be some conflict at the forum. There wasn't. Chuck made his informative report. At the Q and A, four parishioners made impassioned statements—two pro and two anti the ordination of homosexuals. And that was it. The whole issue was hardly ever mentioned again.

Was I responsible for averting a crisis? My feeling is that had there been more outrage, what I did would not have helped. On the other hand, I did what I felt the Lord leading me to do. (I actually had no idea what I would say. The Prayer Book idea came to me spontaneously the moment I stood up to make the announcements. Guidance from the Lord? I believe it was.)

One important take-away, though, is the importance of open discussion. I've learned that when you give people a chance to air their feelings, whatever they are, in private or in public—as in this case—frequently the intensity dissipates.

It's when people feel not heard, feel their feelings aren't important; when they feel shunted aside, discounted by those in authority, that they often react with anger. Or they express that anger to other parishioners in ways that can, in turn, lead to conflict in the parish.

So always take the time to listen. Even when you feel like you don't have the time. Or the interest. Especially when you disagree with them. It will help maintain the smooth tenor of parish life.

QUESTION 56

WHAT HAVE BEEN THE GREATEST JOYS OF YOUR MINISTRY?

First, and always most important to me, has been connecting people to the Lord. That's been the number-one goal of my ministry from the beginning. It's the primary purpose of my life. It's why I feel I was put on earth—followed immediately by what I also know is my call to be Nancy's husband, my children's father, my grandchildren's grandfather, and my brother's brother.

To feel that however God enables me, to somehow hook people up to Jesus is why I answered the call to ministry in the first place. In all these years, I've never varied from that goal.

Everything else I've done as a priest, every other aspect of ministry, though each is important and valid in itself; everything is secondary to this one thing.

If I'm not bringing people to Jesus in some way—through preaching, teaching, leading worship and administering the sacraments, pastoral care, leadership, or even chance encounters—I might as well be leading some secular organization.

The Living God, made known to us in Jesus, by his Spirit present with his people at all times and in all places, has been the heart spring of all I've done as an ordained minister. I can do no good thing without him. But "I can do all things through Christ who strengthens me." So can you.

And from that has come immense joy and satisfaction beyond anything I could have anticipated.

To have led people on the glorious quest to know him and—through our local churches—to make him known in our lives and in all the communities we're a part of is the highest calling we can have as ministers of the gospel.

All we do, we do in his name. All we do must originate with him. All we do can only be effective if inspired and enabled by his Spirit. For us, every day is Pentecost, because we acknowledge and experience and depend on his Spirit for the continuation, the carrying out of his ministry.

We celebrate all the various seasons of the Church Year. But for us in some ways, every day is also Easter Day. Because "Jesus is alive!" is the great pronouncement on which we build our lives and our ministries and our eternal destinies.

We find our other great affirmation in the words of the disciples to Thomas, when they say to him: "We have seen the Lord!"

The world doesn't know it, but it is suffering and dying and languishing in the grip of all manner of false gods because of the intense, yet unsatisfied yearning God has placed deep within every person. It's the yearning to know him. It's the longing for meaning and purpose that can only be satisfied in relationship with him. It's the craving to be loved as only he can love us.

It's up to us to seek the Lord in our lives and ministries. It's our calling, our opportunity, our responsibility and our joy to seek the Lord until we find him. Then, able to say, "I have seen the Lord!" we adopt the ministry of Andrew who brought people who did not know Jesus to discover him and form relationships with him and so to be transformed . . . so they can in turn, with us, can carry out the ministry of transformation wherever the Lord takes us.

We abide in him, so that his life-giving resources can course through us to bring life to those we minister to. But this abiding is not passive. It's an active abiding, characterized by our ongoing dialogue with the Lord. So that we can learn of him and learn *from* him what he wants us to do, where he wants to take us.

Because the ministry of Jesus, by his Spirit, is love, yes. But not a passive love. The love of Jesus is active, throbbing with life, dynamism, Holy Spirit energy; love in action.

Jesus is alive!

We have seen the Lord!

Another declaration of those halcyon hours immediately following the resurrection were spoken by the angel who, according to Mark's version, stayed in the tomb after Jesus left.

The women have come to anoint Jesus' body. They find the stone rolled away. They find that the body of Jesus has disappeared.

They see the angel, "A young man dressed in white," casually sitting there in the tomb. He says:

> Do not be amazed; you are looking for Jesus the Nazarene, who has been crucified. He has risen. He is not here. Behold, here is the place where they laid Him.
>
> But go, tell His disciples and Peter, "He is going before you into Galilee. There you will see Him, just as He said to you." (Mark 16:6–7)

Where do we see him today? How does he make himself known to us now in our lives and in our ministries? We see him, we know him, as he moves out, goes forward, seeks out people where they are, ministers to them with acts of love, deliverance, and mercy. He's always healing, always delivering, always setting people free. He's always on the move, by his Spirit, because there are always more who need him and all he gives them.

The most remarkable thing of all is that when we are open to him and willing to be used by him, he actually does these things through us!

As you and I join him in carrying out his acts of love, not only do we see him as he is, we help others see him, too. We hope, we pray, we trust they see him in us.

QUESTION 57

LOOKING FORWARD: HOW DO WE DEAL WITH THE CHANGING PACE OF THE CHURCH IN TODAY'S CULTURE?

Never in my lifetime has the culture needed the church more than it does today. To the dire societal needs that confront us the gospel of Jesus Christ has the answer. The way of Jesus is our guide for going forward through overwhelming odds to the future God offers us.

What should be our response?

BE OPEN, FLEXIBLE, WILLING TO CHANGE

Studies are being conducted. Books are being written. The place of the church in western culture is in some ways at an all-time low. The organized church, that is. The church is under attack by the culture. And in some cases, justifiably so.

What do we do about it? How do we, as church leaders, handle this radical and unsettling diminishment of our place in the culture?

REMEMBER GOD HAS ALWAYS WORKED WITH REMNANTS

Elijah thought he was the only man left who hadn't turned away from the Lord and embraced idolatry. "Not true, Elijah," the Lord told him. "I have 7,000 in Israel who have not bowed the knee to Baal" (1 Kings 19:18).

Here's what God told Jeremiah, when God's people were lost and wandering due to the lack of caring pastors: "'Then I myself shall gather the remnant of my flock out of all the countries where I have driven them and shall bring them back to their pasture; and they will be fruitful and multiply. I shall also raise up shepherds over them and they will tend them; and they will not be afraid any longer, nor terrified, nor will any be missing,' declares the LORD" (Jeremiah 23:3–4).

That puts the onus on us! If it's poor shepherding that drives some people away from church, it's also positive ministry that brings them back. That understanding needs to drive us to our knees entreating the Spirit to make us the kind of shepherds the Lord needs in these times.

Finally, of course, what was the first church if not a remnant?

A tiny group of Spirit-empowered followers of the resurrected Nazarene, how could they be expected to overcome evil with good? How could this handful of believers be expected to take a new way of thinking and a new way of being into a hardened pagan culture? How could this radical new spiritual species be expected to bring God's light into a world that had known nothing but the darkness of paganism?

But they did. This motley crew of cultural underdogs brought God's revelation of how he would have us live as his people into the jaws of the greatest power of the time. This remnant would overturn the Roman Empire without ever once drawing a sword.

As Paul says, "The same Spirit that raised Christ from the dead lives in us." It's by that same Holy Spirit that so empowered the first believers to build the church in the first place that we are going to build and re-build the church in our time and in the place he plants us.

WHAT'S THE SPIRIT SAYING TO THE CHURCH?

The first thing we as church leaders need to do is discover the Lord's dream for his church in this hour. Then we can move forward to capture the dream and make it a reality.

Study the culture

Learn how your people live, what matters to them. How do they spend their time? What are their priorities?

We were fortunate at St. Matthew's. The majority of our new members were families with young children. This was great! It also presented a problem. For one thing, the young families in our community had very little free time on the weekends.

One young father, who was on the vestry and a deeply committed member, told me: "I commute by train into New York City five days a week. I leave before my children are up in the morning. By the time I get home at night, our youngest is already in bed. Friday night I get home and my wife tells me who we've having dinner with that night. Saturdays she and I divvy up who takes which child to which sporting event. Saturday night: another social event. Sunday is the one day I have where I can actually hang out with my family and get ready for the whole thing to start up again on Monday. For us to all make it to church on a regular basis is a very big commitment for us."

Yet he and his wife and children made that commitment and lived it out week after week.

His story reflected the lives of most of our young members in our commuter community. Something else I learned had to do with priorities.

When I was a boy, growing up in a small town in the Midwest, Sunday morning meant church. Everybody went to church. That's what you did. There weren't all the options for things to do on Sunday that we have now. Believe it or not, no stores were open on Sundays. Only gas stations. Our routine was Sunday morning church, pot roast for lunch, and the afternoon spent at my grandparents' house.

Now you can do everything on Sunday you can do any other day.

We got all these young families as members, but they were attending church only sporadically. Concerned, I put together small focus groups of young parishioners. We met over desert and coffee in various homes.

We asked a series of questions. What drew you to the church? What do you like best? What would you like to see us do that we're not doing now? How was the welcoming process? If you come to church only occasionally—why is that? (My biggest concern.) To which several answered: We love the church. We love being members. But church isn't our only Sunday priority.

A new generation in a culture very different from the one I grew up in. Which poses the question: how can we *be* church for *these* people?

Remember, however the society may change, adapt, evolve, people are still people, with the same needs, hopes, and aspirations.

What do thriving churches and vital congregations have that other churches don't?
They connect their people with God and with each other, especially through dynamic, compelling worship and community-building opportunities—like coffee hours, spring and fall clean-up days, and fun, seasonal, inter-generational events centered on food and sometimes music.

No congregation can be alive apart from a vital and ongoing experience of God's presence among its members. It is from this vivifying relationship with God's Spirit that everything else flows. Churches whose primary concern is enabling people to be full of God are also churches whose pews will be full of God's people.s

These words hold the key. We need God's power manifest in our lives. We have the power. It's the same power that made the pagan world into Christ-believers in the first church. It's the power of the Living God. In him we have the answers for a world searching for hope in the midst of despair.

People are desperately searching, not only for hope; they're searching for *meaning*. They want their lives to count for something. Whether they know it or not, they're searching for God.

A primary lesson from the pandemic is that many more people have come to seek answers—both to why such an overwhelming disaster has struck and how to survive not only COVID-19 but its impact on all parts of society. Never in my lifetime have we as clergy been better positioned by circumstances to direct people to the Lord, source of strength, comfort, courage, and hope.

WORSHIP IS PRIMARY

But it must be prayer-prepared, Spirit-infused worship. Dry, spiritless worship doesn't draw people, it drives them away. Bring God into your worship. Ask him to make himself known to the congregation in these times dedicated to him, in worship that is centered and focused on him.

I've regularly reminded my parishioners that Jesus means literally that when two or three are gathered in his name there he will be, in our midst.

Invite him in. Expect him to be there. Celebrate his presence with you. In the words of Jacob, "Surely the LORD is in this place!" (Genesis 28:19). Trust him to do the rest.

If Jesus is alive in your worship something beautiful is going to happen.

Study the current trends

We can learn from the work that's being done on how the church and society are changing and how some church leaders are successfully responding. Read Phyllis Tickle's landmark *The Great Emergence: How Christianity is Changing and Why* (Grand Rapids: Baker, 2008).

An Episcopalian and lay reader at Washington National Cathedral, she bases her formulating principle on Anglican Bishop Mark Dyer's reminder that "Every five hundred years the Church feels compelled to hold a giant rummage sale . . . and we are living in and through one of those five-hundred-year sales right now."

Taking this historical overview can be reassuring. It reminds us that this kind of thing has happened before—and more than once!

Expanding, Bishop Dyer says: "About every five hundred years the empowered structures of institutionalized Christianity—whatever they may be at the time—must be shattered in order that renewal and new growth may occur" (Tickle, *Great Emergence*, p. 16).

Remember: people are still people

Some things don't change. People—our needs, our passions, our concerns, worries, hopes and dreams—remain basically the same.

Along with all the other things we do, what we need to be continually addressing and constructively re-addressing in our preaching, teaching, pastoral care, and interpersonal interchanges with our parishioners are the timeless, recurring problems that make us human.

Plus, we need to be willing to question everything we know about the church. At the ordinations of two deacons, Bishop Knisely of Rhode Island said, "I ended my excellent preparation at Berkeley Divinity School in the late 1980s to serve the church of the 1970s." Addressing the ordinands, he added: "You are being ordained to serve in a church that is passing away. The question: How do we learn to preach a gospel not for then but for now, for today; for this moment in time?"

The Bishop was right. The church we know is *always* changing, *always* in process, sometimes in barely perceptible ways, sometimes overtly.

As church leaders what we need to do is discover the Lord's dream for his church *in this hour*. Then we can move forward to capture the dream and make it a reality.

Remember who we are

In the words of Archbishop of Canterbury Justin Welby, in a sermon preached at Virginia Theological Seminary:

> Within these walls have been felt every sorrow and joy that can assail the human heart. Within these walls people have cried out for help and their cries have been heard. Within these walls we who have received mercy are called to give others mercy. Let this place form and shape us so that we go forth carrying the torch of unity, forgiveness, and hope that we find here. Church is a place where a wandering throng of pilgrims are transformed into a band of light-bearers. May we go forth and burn with fire—the fire of the living God!

QUESTION 58

HOW CAN THE CHURCH MEET
THE CRISES OF THE TIMES?

The church is the only institution that by call and function exists to provide the antidote to the culture's greatest needs, some of which have become more daunting than at any time in history. Whatever the magnitude of the problem, our response as God's people should be not defeat and not complacency, but engagement.

THE NEEDS

Alienation
To the cultural increase in isolation, alienation, and polarization, we offer the warmth, acceptance, mutual caring, support, and trust of committed, intimate Christian fellowship. (See small groups, above.) Our fellowship, as the community of believers, when we are at our best naturally lifts those who may initially feel alienated into a place of belonging and emotional safety. It happens to all of us when we feel loved as the Lord would have us love each other.

In the words of Peter's call to the church: "Fervently love one another from the heart." (1 Peter 22b)

Immorality
To the increasing lowering of moral standards—as in, students cheating on their exams and, when apprehended, saying they thought it was all right as long as they didn't get caught; as in, parents paying great sums of money in bribes to get their children in the schools of their choice; as in,

the obvious lying, greed, and sexual impropriety that keeps being uncovered and graphically reported in the media—to all these things, the church offers, the church lifts high, an option: the highest ethical standards. Morals. Values. Honesty. Honor. Even—how rare and how unpopular is this concept in today's society—purity. We can't avoid it: the church is called to raise the moral standard of the country. (Which is why betrayal of these standards by clergy is that much more devastating.)

We're called to model purity and another culturally unpopular, virtually unknown word, a word that nonetheless characterizes our God and that he should, by rights, be able to apply to his people.

Holiness is the word. It's a word ignored, so forgotten, so virtually lost in the world we know today. A lot of people confronted with the concept of holy living would respond with contempt. Holy? You're joking!

When it comes to our being holy, the holy God is not joking.

Paul wrote to Timothy and the first-generation church words that apply to the church of today: "God . . . has called us with a holy calling" (2 Timothy 1:9b).

In Ephesians Paul expands his definition: "He chose us in Him before the foundation of the world, that we should be holy and blameless before Him" (Ephesians 1:4b)

What is this holiness that defines our God and ought, according to him, apply also to us? It's worth some serious study.

Hate

I've already addressed the church's necessary response to White supremacy, racism, anti-Semitism, and intolerance of any and all kinds. It's our unity in Christ Jesus.

Here's Paul on unity: "For just as we have many members in one body and all the members do not have the same function, so we who are many, are one body in Christ, and individually members of one another" (Romans 12:4–5).

And Jesus, in his valedictory remarks to the disciples the night before he died, prayed to the Father. He prayed for them—and for us: "I do not ask in behalf of these alone, but for those also who believe in Me through their words; that they may all be one; even as Thou, Father, are in Me and I in Thee, that they also may be in Us; that the world may believe that Thou didst send me" (John 17:20–21).

It does provide a powerful witness, doesn't it, this unity we affirm and celebrate and ideally demonstrate?

Global warming
Here, too, we have an obligation to lead the way in cherishing God's glorious creation. He made Adam and Eve stewards of the Garden. He has never revoked that order. It's our responsibility and our honor to do all we can to help save the environment.

And the natural order shares with us the drastic results of the fall. We read in Romans: "For we know the whole creation groans and suffers the pains of childbirth together until now" (Romans 8:22). In other words, creation also suffered because of Adam and Eve's fall from grace and expulsion from the Garden. The Lord warned that he was introducing thorns and thistles where before there had been only luscious edibles. He told Eve giving birth would be painful. He told Adam that instead of simply harvesting the food grown without human aid in the Garden, now he'd have to sweat and strain to grow crops from an often rocky and sometimes inhospitable soil.

In the meantime, as the people of God, we have a responsibility to nurture, care for, and cherish nature—which means we must do all we can do to save the environment.

Meanwhile, we need to learn what creation has to teach us. In the introduction to a book of Celtic spirituality we read:

> In the Celtic tradition, God is understood as speaking through two books: The Bible and creation. Influenced by the wisdom tradition of the Old Testament and the mysticism of John's Gospel, Celtic spirituality sees creation not simply as gift, but as a self-giving of God whose image is to be found deep within all living things. Sin may obscure God's living presence, but never erases it. The divine voice can be heard speaking through all created things.
>
> For centuries, the view that the world is alienated from God has damaged our understanding of creation, but today, as more people are recovering their Celtic heritage, we are again learning to reverence creation as the dwelling place of God. (J. Philip Newell, *The Book of Creation: An Introduction to Celtic Christianity*. Mahwah, NJ: Paulist, 1999.)

To love God is to love his creation.

It's therefore obvious that as God's people we need to take our place in the front ranks of everything that can be done to save the planet.

Violence

What about mass shootings? As Christians, we abhor and must do all we can to resist this plague of gun-related violence.

We need to do everything we can to call for stricter gun laws, demand the removal of military arms from the hands of private citizens, and require psychiatric testing of certain suspect gun buyers.

We also need to pray. This is not a hollow suggestion. Again, it's Paul who reminds us that we are locked in a battle with evil. Satan exists. We live in a fallen realm where he and his demons hold sway.

Paul shows us how to counteract evil:

> Finally, be strong in the Lord, and in the strength of His might. Put on the full armor of God, that you may be able to stand firm against the schemes of the devil. For our struggle is not against flesh and blood, but against the powers, against the world forces of this darkness, against the spiritual forces of wickedness in the heavenly places.
>
> Stand firm therefore, having girded your loins with truth and having put on the breastplate of righteousness.
>
> And having shod your feet with the preparation of the Gospel of peace; in addition to all, taking up the shield of faith with which you will be able to extinguish all the flaming missiles of the Evil one. And take the helmet of salvation, and the sword of the Spirit, which is the word of God. *With all prayer and petition pray at all times in the Spirit.* (Ephesians 6:10–18a)

Racism

Racism, the assumed supremacy of one race over another, is obviously un-godly. In the beginning, God made humanity, *all* humanity, in his own image. Jesus laid down his life for the *whole* world, not for those of some races but not for others.

One of the reasons Jesus so enraged the status-conscious Jewish establishment is because he hung out with people considered to be of the lowest social order—lepers, prostitutes, street people, and even gentiles, people of other races.

Isaiah prophetically affirmed the future emancipation of the slaves in the U.S., Great Britain, and other countries with these words: "Is this not the fast that I choose: to loose the bonds of injustice, to undo the thongs of the yoke, to let the oppressed go free? And break every yoke" (Isaiah 58:6).

The church is called to be today's repairer of every breach that exists between races, creeds, and religions.

And the apostle Paul laid down the anti-racist manifesto of the church when he wrote: "There is no longer Jew or Greek, there is no longer slave or free, there is no longer male and female; for all of you are one in Jesus Christ" (Galatians 3:2). Paul went on to tell the church that we have the ministry of *reconciliation*. We are to actively reconcile ourselves to one another, whatever differences might exist. Meanwhile, Jesus calls us not merely to tolerate racial differences; he would have us climb a rung higher on the ladder of reconciliation and actually value, even cherish, racial differences. For surely if God glories in his creation, *all* his creation, so should we. "And God saw everything that he had made, and behold it was very good" (Genesis 1:31).

OUR RESPONSE

Pray

What this says to me is that we need to raise up and encourage the ministry and practice of intercessory prayer in our churches. We need to issue a call to prayer. See if there are those in your church who feel called to pray. Teach the meaning, the power, and the necessity of prayer—individually and in groups.

Pray for the church. Pray for each other. Pray for the nation and all in authority. Pray for hate-fueled violence to stop. Pray for an end to racism. Pray for the healing and salvation of the planet. Pray for revival, for a mighty move of God to bring people to repentance that goodness might reign at last—that the afflicted might be healed, the broken-hearted comforted, those who are captive to fear, inequality, brutality, inequality, misery of any kind set free.

Pray and lead your people in praying consistently, persistently, passionately for the things listed above and for any others the Lord puts on your—and their hearts—to pray for. The ministry of intercessory prayer is too often neglected. Make it a priority. You'll see the results.

Consider the words of Watchman Nee.

Apostle and prophet of the church in China, persecuted and imprisoned by the Chinese government, Watchman Nee spent the last twenty years of his life in prison, where he died in 1972. His words ring with relevance for the church today.

In his landmark *What Shall This Man Do?*—a handbook for Christian service—Watchman Nee relates the ministry of prayer to our call and work as ministers of the gospel.

> Prayer is the present exercising of my will in God's favor; declaring that his will shall be done. For this is true prayer, that what God makes known, we express. . . . This ministry of being God's outlet is our greatest possible work. God shows what he wants. We stand and ask, and God acts from heaven. This is true prayer, and this is what we must see fully expressed. . . . With the Kingdom in view, all we have and all we do must be set for the will of God. God needs this. He must have a few throughout the nations who hold on in prayer, and who, by driving a wedge into the power of the enemy, bring in the next age. That is overcoming. Whether the members may be many or few, may God maintain our strength to work for him in deep, strong, prevailing prayer . . . .
>
> THE PURPOSE OF GOD IN HIS CHURCH IS GOING TO BE ACCOMPLISHED. . . . THE VISION OF THE HOLY CITY, MADE READY AS A BRIDE ADORNED FOR HER HUSBAND, WILL UNFAILINGLY COME TO PASS, AND WE SHALL SEE IT. . . . IT IS SETTLED IN HEAVEN." (*What Shall This Man Do?* Wheaton, IL: Tyndale House, 1978, Portions of pp. 201, 203, 269.)

So may it be on earth.

ACCEPT THE CHALLENGE; EMBRACE THE CALL

Other prophetic voices through the years have underscored the need to embrace the call of boldly continuing to carry the message of Jesus to the world. Two stand out in light of where we are now; two voices to two very different generations which speak equally to the needs of today.

Walter Rauschenbusch in the early twentieth century exploded the complacency of the mainline church with his then-revolutionary concept of "the social gospel." His basic message was simple. Standing in the tradition of the ancient Hebrew prophets, the tradition of Jesus, Rauschenbusch proclaimed that where the local church is, we should see Jesus. If Jesus is present we will also see changed lives, which in turn result in compassion pouring forth into the lives and circumstances of the neediest among us. The result? A reformation of the social order.

Rauschenbusch wrote:

Think what it would signify to a local community if all sincere Christian people in it should interpret their obligation in social terms; if they should seek not only their own salvation, but the reign of God in their town; if they should cultivate the habit of seeing a divine sacredness in every personality, should assist in creating the economic foundations for solidarity, and, if, as Christians, they should champion the weak in their own community. We need a power of renewal in our American communities that will carry across the coming transition, and social Christianity can supply it by directing the force of the old faith of our forebears to the new social tasks. (Walter Rauschenbusch, *The Social Principles of Jesus.* Philadelphia: The Methodist Book Concern, 1916, p. 196.)

Rauschenbusch launched the Social Gospel movement that initiated mission and outreach ministries in local churches, many of which before Rauschenbusch had barely noticed the mission needs in their own neighborhoods. Like a theological Charles Dickens, he caught the hearts of thousands of people with his eloquent plea to help those who could not help themselves.

Nothing has changed in terms of our calling. The needs still exist today, aggravated by the awful economic effects of the pandemic on the lives of so many who were already living on the edge.

Rauschenbusch, still speaking to us as to his first readers, goes on:

Jesus was the initiator of the Kingdom of God. It is a real thing, now in operation. It is within us, and among us, gaining ground in our intellectual life and in our social institutions. It overlaps and penetrates all existing organizations, raising them to a higher level when they are good, resisting them when they are evil, quietly revolutionizing the old social order and changing it into the new. It suffers terrible reverses; we are in the midst of one now. But after a time, it may become apparent that a master hand has turned the situation and laid the basis for victory on the wrecks of defeat." (Ibid.)

Seeing the explosion of immorality, polarization, anger, continued racial inequality, and a rising generation that seemingly has little time for so-called organized religion, Rauschenbusch speaks directly to us today.

He closes with these words of hope:

The Kingdom of God is always coming; you can never lay your hand on it and say, "It is here." But such fragmentary realizations of it as we have, alone make life worth living. The memories which are still sweet and dear when the fire begins to die in the ashes, are the memories of days when we lived fully in the Kingdom of Heaven, toiling for it, suffering for it, and feeling the stirring of the godlike and eternal life within us. (Ibid., p. 197)

In a contemporary voice, we hear Tim Keller's seeming affirmation of Rauschenbusch's long-ago call to the social expression and manifestation of the gospel. Says Keller: "Christianity will not be attractive enough to win influence except through sacrificial service to all people, regardless of their beliefs." (Quoted in Gabe Lyons, *The Next Christians*. Portland: Multnomah Books, 2010.)

Another current voice calling us to embrace the call to transform and even save the culture, is that of Oz Guinness. In his *Renaissance: The Power of the Gospel However Dark the Times* (Downers Grove, IL: IVP, 2014), he balances an immense challenge to the church—that we usher in a new spiritual renaissance (reformation)—with the ever present, ever empowering, ever enabling power of God.

Near the end of the book, he shifts from seeing our call as not simply to help save Christian civilization, but with what he sees as the survival of humanity.

> There is no fact that the stakes are high, the urgency is great, and the gravity is plain. We are entering a crunch generation for the world. The global era is raising questions for humanity that are unprecedented and that will call into question the very future of mankind and of our planet home. Much of the world as Christians have known it for centuries has gone, and what the world of tomorrow will be like we do not know and cannot say.
>
> But those who know and trust God need not fear. The recovery of the integrity and effectiveness of faith in the advanced modern world is a titanic task that boggles the mind and daunts the heart. But God is greater than all, so God may be trusted in all situations. The time has come to trust God, move out, sharing and demonstrating the good news, following his call and living out our callings in every area of our lives, and then leave the outcome to him.
>
> Transforming engagement in the power of the gospel will never prove vain . . . .
>
> We may be in the dark about our times, but we are never in the dark about God. Whatever the future holds, we are walking in the light with our Lord, so followers of Jesus must have the courage and the faith to work for a new renaissance in our time. So let

there be no fear, no alarmism, nor despondency, nor nostalgia. Instead, let us look up and so act with faith as to say with our prayers as with our lives, "Let a thousand flowers bloom!" (Ibid.)

Yes! The Lord is on the move. Unquestionably the times are dark. There have been dark times before. And every time, ultimately, in every age, his church has triumphed. He has triumphed. As we go forward with him, our greatest challenge becomes our greatest adventure.

GLOSSARY OF TERMS

ANGLICAN

A person who is a communicant of any church (such as the Episcopal Church) that is part of the worldwide Anglican Communion and owes its identity to a historical and liturgical relationship to the Church of England. Traditionally England was Angleland, or the land of the Angles, one of the Germanic tribes who settled there early in the Christian era; therefore, the Church of England is also ecclesia anglicana, or the Anglican Church.

THE BOOK OF COMMON PRAYER

The authorized prayer book of the Episcopal Church. It contains the regular services appointed for public worship, including the Holy Eucharist (Communion), the daily offices, and principle feasts and fasts of the church. It also contains the pastoral offices of baptism, marriage, and burial; Episcopal services; the collects; and the Psalter. In the first Book of Common Prayer, composed by Archbishop Thomas Cranmer in 1549, the complicated rites of the medieval church were gathered into a single book for clergy and laity; henceforth, worship would be conducted in the vernacular instead of Latin. The first American prayer book was ratified in 1789 after the Revolutionary War, with new editions authorized in 1892, 1928, and 1979. The prayer book is essential to the character of the Episcopal Church because it holds together congregations with very different styles of worship within the church's broader traditions of Christian belief and practice.

PROTESTANT EPISCOPAL CHURCH IN THE UNITED STATES OF AMERICA

One of the official names of the Episcopal Church. The other being the Episcopal Church in the United States of America. The Episcopal Church is a province of the Anglican Communion, and traces its roots to the settlement of the Church of England in Virginia in 1607. While Virginia remained the center of its strength in the seventeenth and eighteenth centuries, Anglicanism spread throughout all thirteen colonies prior to the American Revolution. After war severed ties with England, clergy and lay people were forced to reorganize the institutional life of the church. Samuel Seabury was consecrated as the first American bishop in 1784, and thanks to the leadership of Philadelphia Bishop William White , a new denomination was established in 1789. It was called the Protestant Episcopal Church in the United States of America-"Protestant" signifying its Reformation heritage, "Episcopal" designating its national status. The Episcopal Church now contains over a hundred diocese in Europe, Central America, and South America, as well as in the United States. It is governed by a bicameral General Convention that meets every three years. In 1967 the General convention approved a preamble to the church's constitution, recognized recognizing "The Episcopal Church" as the customary form of the denomination's name.

RECTOR

Chief sacramental, liturgical, and administrative leader of a parish, who is called by and accountable to the vestry. The rector calls and manages both clergy and lay staffs. The term is derived from the Latin word for "to lead" or "to rule."

RECTORY

House owned by the parish in which the rector lives.